Karen Silva

...RONGHOLDS...

IT IS SAID THAT IN THE PERSIAN GULF WAR, SADDAM HUSsein would fire Scud missiles and then turn on CNN to find out where they hit. In turn, the allies came back with smart bombs, which pinpointed exactly the smokestacks or windows they were supposed to strike. I believe it is time Christian people begin smart-bomb praying.

This book uncovers the wiles of the devil and exposes the prayer targets that will force the enemy to release millions of unsaved souls now held captive. I am excited that God has given us a marvelous new tool for effective spiritual warfare!

C. Peter Wagner

EDITED BY C. PETER WAGNER

BREAKING STRONGHOLDS IN YOUR CITY

HOW TO USE SPIRITUAL MAPPING TO MAKE YOUR PRAYERS MORE STRATEGIC, EFFECTIVE AND TARGETED

Regal Books
A Division of Gospel Light
Ventura, California, U.S.A.

Published by Regal Books
A Division of Gospel Light
Ventura, California, U.S.A.
Printed in U.S.A.

Please note that the views expressed by each individual contributor may not agree with the
views of the other writers in this work.

Library of Congress Cataloging-in-Publication Data
Breaking strongholds in your city : how to identify the enemy's territory in your city and
pray for its deliverance / C. Peter Wagner, editor.
   p. cm.
   Includes bibliographical references and index.
   ISBN 0-8307-1597-5
   1. Spiritual warfare.   2. Devil.   3. A.D. 2000 Movement.   4. City missions.   I. Wag-
     ner, C. Peter.
BT981.B654   1993
235'.4—dc20
                                                  93-12065
                                                   CIP
1 2 3 4 5 6 7 8 9 10 / X3.11 / KP / 99 98 97 96 95 94 93

Rights for publishing this book in other languages are contracted by Gospel
Literature International (GLINT). GLINT also provides technical help for the
adaptation, translation, and publishing of Bible study resources and books in
scores of languages worldwide. For further information, contact GLINT, Post
Office Box 488, Rosemead, California, 91770, U.S.A., or the publisher.

Lovingly dedicated to
Becky Wagner

Contents

RONGHOLDS...

PART III: APPLICATION

Introduction

ONGHOLDS...

by C. Peter Wagner

THIS IS ONE OF THOSE INTRODUCTIONS YOU WILL DO well to read before going on with the rest of the book! Spiritual mapping is such a new subject that few who pick up this book will have had much background understanding to prepare the way. For those who have become informed on strategic-level spiritual warfare it will not be so difficult because a mental paradigm has already been established. For others, however, this book will be an entry point for tuning in to what I consider one of the most important things the Spirit is saying to the churches in the 1990s, and this introduction will be extremely helpful for that process.

THE EMERGENCE OF SPIRITUAL MAPPING

I personally never heard the term "spiritual mapping" in the 1970s or the 1980s. As recent as 1990, in a meeting of a small organization called the Spiritual Warfare Network, I heard Pastor Dick Bernal of Jubilee Christian Center tell how the leaders and intercessors of his church had attempted to identify the spiritual principalities over the different cities and regions around the San Francisco Bay area. Others in the meeting questioned the wisdom of doing such a thing, and quite a lively discussion followed. I suppose someone had been using the term previously, but at least for me this was my first introduction to the concept.

A rapid succession of events followed, and the upshot involved the Spiritual Warfare Network becoming integrated into the United Prayer Track of the A.D. 2000 Movement. The A.D. 2000 Movement has been raised up by God as the chief force for catalyzing the multiple churches, agencies, ministries and denominations around the world for a concerted effort to complete the task of world evangelization, at least as much as possible, by the year 2000. It is a grassroots organization and its activities are delegated to 10 separate interest tracks or resource networks. My current responsibility is to lead the A.D. 2000 United Prayer Track, which is building a global prayer base to undergird the efforts of all the other tracks and the evangelistic movement as a whole.

The most prominent unit within the United Prayer Track is the Spiritual Mapping Division led by George Otis, Jr., co-coordinator of the Prayer Track. The establishment of this division has raised the profile of this new field of ministry to worldwide dimensions. We in the A.D. 2000 Movement are no longer discussing whether we *should* do spiritual mapping. We are now concentrating our energies on *how to do it well.*

Filtering Out the Flakes

It is no secret that intercession, spiritual warfare, dealing with the demonic, and now spiritual mapping tend to attract more than their share of flakes. The authors of this book, the Spiritual Warfare Network, the United Prayer Track, the Spiritual Mapping Division, and the A.D. 2000 Movement take seriously their responsibility of filtering out the flakes as much as possible and building an accountability system, which will help keep us from becoming flaky ourselves. We are striving to lay biblical, theological and pastorally sensitive ministry foundations for spiritual mapping with excellence and integrity. We will probably make mistakes ourselves, but hopefully when we do we will learn from them and promptly correct them.

WHY THIS BOOK?

Five years, or even 2 years from this writing we will certainly know more about spiritual mapping than we do today. Nevertheless, in the providence of God, He has been raising up a fairly small group of people from many parts of the world who have actually been doing spiritual mapping for up to 20 years and have accumulated considerable experience.

I believe that more than any other book I have written, this one emerged from the immediate leading of God. I had planned on doing a series of three books on prayer beginning with *Warfare Prayer* and *Prayer Shield*, both of which Regal Books has now published. The third was to be a book on prayer relating to the local church. All three are for the purpose of seeing strategic, targeted prayer contribute toward the acceleration of world evangelization. But God interrupted me and I strongly sensed that I was to do this book on spiritual mapping next because God wanted church leaders to have a practical guidebook for implementing what the Spirit is saying to the churches about spiritual mapping now.

When I began to raise the objection that I did not know enough about spiritual mapping to do a whole book, God seemed to become more specific. I clearly recall in my prayer time in a motel in Portland, Oregon, I sensed an anointing from the Lord and in less than 45 minutes I had written out on my yellow pad the basic outline of the book you now have. Undoubtedly other Christian leaders in the world could match the insights and wisdom of these authors, but I doubt if many would surpass them. Those who contributed to this book are from the United States, Sweden, Guatemala and Argentina. Each one of them began spiritual mapping without training or contacts with others who were doing it. Now they are communicating with each other through the Spiritual Warfare Network, and they are both amazed and gratified that for years they had each been receiving similar instructions from the Lord.

MEET THE CONTRIBUTORS

What is spiritual mapping? Several of our experts have given their definitions, all of which reinforce and complement the others. The nontechnical condensed definition is: *An attempt to see our* (fill in the region to be mapped) *as it really is, not as it appears to be.* This comes from George Otis, Jr., who through his works such as *The Last of the Giants* (Chosen Books) and his worldwide ministry with The Sentinel Group and the A.D. 2000 United Prayer Track, is regarded by many including myself as the top leader of the field. I was delighted when George agreed to contribute the first chapter and provide an overview of the philosophy of spiritual mapping in general.

As the founder and president of Generals of Intercession, Cindy Jacobs excels both in the teaching of strategic-level spiritual warfare and in leading pastors and intercessors to actually practice it out in the field. Her chapter on strongholds will clarify many questions that are frequently raised. Cindy's book, *Possessing the Gates of the Enemy* (Chosen Books), is an enlightening training manual for militant intercession, and has been highly acclaimed.

Kjell (pronounced "Shell") Sjöberg has been known for his ministry of strategic-level spiritual intercession, prophetic prayer actions and spiritual mapping longer than any of the other authors. His book, *Winning the Prayer War* (Sovereign World), breaks new ground for us in this field. No one else I know could relate spiritual mapping to prophetic prayer actions with the insight and field experience that Kjell brings to his chapter.

Along with my chapter on "The Visible and the Invisible," which I consider one of the most important essays I have written in recent years, this group provides the "Principles" section of this book. For the "Practice" section I have chosen three practitioners from three different nations, each of whom is deeply engaged in spiritual mapping and each of whom began with virtually no help, instruction or models from others.

The Practice Section
Harold Caballeros, the pastor of El Shaddai Church in Guatemala, which currently counts the president of Guatemala and his family among their active membership, is the first pastor in whose personal study I found more textbooks on archaeology than commentaries on Romans. Not that Harold neglects informed biblical exposition in his pastoral ministry, but he takes very seriously the need for understanding the spiritual forces that have shaped his community since the time of the Mayan empire. His chapter will take you right to the heart of the issue.

Bob Beckett has perhaps been able to monitor more closely than any of the others the actual results of spiritual mapping and strategic-level spiritual warfare in his local church, The Dwelling Place Family Church, and in his community of Hemet, California. When I teach my course on this subject at Fuller, I ask Bob to do the lecture on spiritual mapping, then I take the

---

We do not regard spiritual mapping as an end in itself. We see a cause-and-effect relationship between the faithfulness of God's people in prayer and the coming of His Kingdom.

---

entire class out to Hemet for a spiritual mapping field trip, which Bob leads. When you read his chapter, you will get a glimpse of what our Fuller students are learning through him.

I mention Victor Lorenzo frequently in my book *Warfare Prayer* (Regal Books), because Argentina has emerged as our chief field laboratory for testing strategic-level spiritual warfare, and Victor has been a key participant in the process. As he explains, he has worked together a great deal with Cindy Jacobs. Of all our authors, Victor has uncovered more specific information on the enemy's forces in a given city, including discovering the proper names of some of the territorial spirits. The evangelistic outcome has been gratifying.

The Application

The final section, "Application," is included to help answer one of the most frequent questions I get: How does a pastor from Pumphandle, Nebraska, who is not a Kjell Sjöberg or a Cindy Jacobs, go about doing spiritual mapping? Mark McGregor fits the description. He is a committed Christian, but a lay person, a full-time computer programmer who desires to serve the Lord wherever he can. He is the only contributor not affiliated with the Spiritual Warfare Network. In order to map his city of Seattle, he simply took the list of questions from John Dawson's *Taking Our Cities for God* (Creation House), and dug out data from books and other information available to the public such as in libraries, city halls or historical societies. This is not meant to minimize Mark, but if he can do it, so can you. Read his chapter to get the general idea of the kind of information needed.

Just gathering the data is an essential step, but not enough. Here is where people with specific spiritual gifts, experience and maturity in the Lord need to step in. One of those is Bev Klopp, for years a recognized intercessor and a member of the intercession team for the Spiritual Warfare Network. Using her gift of discernment of spirits along with years of experience in praying for Seattle, Bev provides a model for interpreting the data and identifying the targets. When you are ready to move from information gathering to the battlefield, be sure you have some Bev Klopps on your team.

In the last chapter, I have gleaned from what the others have said in the book and put together a suggested spiritual mapping instrument, which some may find helpful as they move into this productive area of ministry.

WHAT GOOD IS SPIRITUAL MAPPING?

As many of our contributors stress, we do not regard spiritual mapping as an end in itself. However, we do believe it is God's desire for us to pray, "Your kingdom come. Your will be done on earth as it is in heaven" (Matt. 6:10). We also see a cause-and-effect relationship between the faithfulness of God's people in prayer and the coming of His Kingdom. When God's will is done on earth we see lost people saved; sick people healed; poor people with sufficient essentials; an end to wars, fighting and bloodshed; oppressed people liberated; just governments; fair and equitable business practices; harmony among races, just to mention some of the benefits.

Many Christian leaders feel that up to now the prayer ministry in our churches has not been of the most powerful kind. I love the way George Otis, Jr., expresses this:

> Although prayer is routinely acknowledged as an important component of global evangelization efforts, these expressions are more often the product of religious habit than they are reflections of any genuine conviction. Like other religious peoples around the world, we pray because we are hesitant to embark on significant undertakings without first acknowledging our familiar deity. Whether or not God will respond to specific requests is of less importance than insuring we have not caused offense by neglecting to inform Him of our intentions. In this sense, prayer is more superstitious and prophylactic than it is supernatural and procreative.[1]

As Bob Beckett says in his chapter, much of our praying has been like Saddam Hussein launching Scud missiles. He had little idea what he was aiming them at, and consequently they did very little good. Those who pray to deliver people from demonic oppression have long since learned that, generally speaking, results are much greater when the evil spirits are identified and specifically commanded to leave in the name of Jesus rather than ministering with a vague prayer such as, "Lord, if there are any spirits here we command them all to leave in Your name." We suspect that the same may be true of praying deliverance over neighborhoods, cities or nations. Spiritual mapping is simply a tool to allow us to be more specific, and hopefully more powerful, in praying for our community.

George Otis, Jr. says, "Those who take the time both to talk and to listen to God before launching their ministry ventures will not only find themselves in the right place at the right time, but they will also know what to do when they get there."[2] Those of us who are developing the theme of spiritual mapping are attempting to increase our ability to hear from God and to communicate to others what we are hearing as accurately as possible.

IS SPIRITUAL MAPPING BIBLICAL?

Several of our authors address the issue of biblical basis for spiritual mapping. It is not my purpose here to reiterate their arguments except to say that all of us who contributed to this book see ourselves as biblical Christians and none of us would so much as consider recommending an area of ministry to the Body of Christ if we were not thoroughly convinced that what we are teaching is the will of God and does not in any way violate scriptural teaching. We are personally convinced that spiritual mapping is biblical and are proceeding from that premise.

At the same time, we are not ignorant of the fact that other brothers and sisters of high Christian integrity will disagree with us. Several have recently published such thoughts in articles and books. We thank God for our informed critics and bless them. For one thing, they have picked up some errors, misstatements or exaggerations we have made and we are in the process of correcting them. For another thing, we feel that even our less informed critics keep us on our toes and help us sharpen what we say and what we do. In no case do we have a desire to enter into polemics and attempt to refute our critics. We have no inclination to make ourselves look good by making other brothers and sisters in Christ look bad, and you will find none of that in this book.

We are acutely aware that spiritual mapping, along with

strategic-level spiritual warfare, are relatively new innovations being introduced into the Body of Christ. We happen to feel that we are being led by the Holy Spirit, but even so, well-known social scientific laws of diffusion of innovation inexorably will be in effect. Any innovation typically draws early adopters, then middle adopters and finally late adopters. In many cases some refuse ever to adopt the innovation, as the existence of the International Flat Earth Society well demonstrates. Spiritual mapping is currently in the early adopter stage and it is the stage that, predictably, stimulates the most heated controversy. The knee-jerk Christian reaction when opposing any innovation is to say, "It is not biblical," as some did when the Sunday School was first introduced and as some did for the abolition of slavery.

Biblical and Archaeological Examples

An example of spiritual mapping is seen in Ezekiel 4:1-3 where God instructs Ezekiel to make a map of the city of Jerusalem on a clay tablet, then "lay siege against it." Obviously, this refers to spiritual, not conventional, warfare.

I mention this because some research has turned up what is regarded by archaeologists as the first known map of a city, the city of Nippur, the ancient cultural center of Sumer. It is on a well-preserved clay tablet, undoubtedly similar to the one Ezekiel used. The features on the map, drawn around 1500 B.C., constitute what we today would call spiritual mapping. In the center of the city is written "the place of *Enlil*." It is said that in the city "dwelt the air god, *Enlil*, the leading deity of the Sumerian pantheon."[3] We would identify it as the territorial spirit over Sumer.

Other buildings on the map include the *Ekur*, Sumer's most renowned temple; the *Kagal Nanna*, or the gate of *Nanna*, the Sumerian moon god; the *Kagal Nergal* or the gate of *Nergal* who was the king of the nether world and husband of the goddess *Ereshkigal*, the *Eshmah* or "Lofty Shrine" on the outskirts of the city and many more.[4]

One more interesting fact. You will see in Victor Lorenzo's chapter that part of the evil, occultic design of the Argentine city of La Plata involved intentionally breaking the usual Latin American pattern by not having the streets run in the direction of the cardinal points: north, south, east and west. The same thing happened in Nippur! Assyriologist Samuel Kramer observes, "The map was oriented, not due north-south, but more or less at a 45-degree angle."[5]

Apparently some historical precedents to spiritual mapping exist.

Does This Glorify Satan?

Uncovering the wiles of the devil can become so fascinating that we can begin to focus attention on the enemy rather than on God. This must be avoided at all costs. If we do it, we play into the enemy's hands. The chief purpose of Satan's existence is to prevent God from being glorified. His motivation for this is that he wants the glory for himself. If he possibly can, he will deceive the servants of God, diverting them into activities that end up exalting the creature rather than the Creator.

Each of the contributors to this book is mature enough spiritually and experienced enough in practical spiritual warfare that they fully recognize Satan's desires and they give him no satisfaction. They agree that the response to the danger is not to back off and leave the battleground to Satan. The response is to move ahead as aggressively as possible to uncover the desires, strategies, techniques and weapons of the enemy. The research helping us do this is no more intended to glorify Satan than cancer research is intended to glorify cancer. But the more we know about the nature, cause, characteristics and effects of cancer the better is our chance to eradicate it. Years ago, for example, smallpox research exposed much of our ignorance concerning smallpox, and as a result millions and millions of human lives were saved. Smallpox was not glorified, it was defeated.

Greater than the danger of glorifying the enemy is to be ignorant of the enemy. I like the way William Kumuyi, the African coordinator for the A.D. 2000 Movement and a leader in the Spiritual Warfare Network says it: "The Enemy often takes advantage of our ignorance. If you are fighting an unseen enemy who is determined to destroy you and you are not vigilant, and you do not even know that there is a fight going on, the Enemy will take advantage of that ignorance and defeat you in the middle of the battle."[6]

C. S. Lewis did not write *The Screwtape Letters* to glorify Satan or demons such as Wormwood, but rather to give us tools so we could better combat them in Jesus' name. Books such as this one on spiritual mapping are designed for the same purpose.

NOT ALL ARE CALLED TO THE FRONTLINES

It is only natural, while reading a book such as this, to say, "I want to be like Harold Caballeros" or "I want to be like Bob Beckett." Nothing is wrong with desiring to do the things they do, *so long as God has called you to do it.* But God does not call everyone to frontline spiritual warfare any more than He calls everyone to be a public evangelist or a cross-cultural missionary. For example, only a tiny percentage of those in the Air Force actually fly the warplanes or even ride in them as crew members. The same applies to spiritual warfare.

The *whole* church is an army and in the midst of a spiritual battle. We *all* should sing, "Onward Christian Soldiers." But not everyone in the army is assigned to the frontlines. Those on the frontlines need those who stay behind and those who stay behind need those on the frontlines.

THE LAW OF WARFARE

When the children of Israel were preparing to take the Promised Land, God gave them the law of warfare. This is important for us today when we realize that God was preparing them for *spiritual* warfare, not *conventional* warfare. What conventional army ever defeated a city by marching around it *X* number of times and blowing horns? I believe these laws of warfare as recorded in Deuteronomy 20 are valid today.

Several whole categories of vigorous grown men who might otherwise have been considered as warriors in Joshua's army were specifically to be excluded from the frontlines. Those who had just built a new house were to go back. Also those who had planted a new vineyard and those who were engaged to a woman but not yet married. Some reasoning is given in the text for each one of these exclusions. But then it goes on to say that those who are "fearful and fainthearted" should also return (see Deut. 20:8).

Significantly, in my opinion, no indication of rebuke or disappointment is recorded. Apparently their rightful place was at home, not at war.

This same law of warfare was applied later to Gideon. Gideon started with 32,000 potential warriors. Of these, 22,000 were fearful or fainthearted and they were encouraged to go home. Then God called only 300 out of the 10,000 who would otherwise have been eligible. They were not the biggest, the strongest, the youngest, the fastest runners, the most experienced, the best sword fighters or even the bravest. In His own way, God sovereignly called 300 to go and He called 9,700 *not to go.*

This is the way the Body of Christ is intended to operate. God gifts and calls only a few to be public evangelists and to preach the gospel to crowds from platforms. God calls only a few to leave their homes and families and to move in as missionaries to a foreign country and a foreign culture. They need the rest of us who do not go on the platforms or to other countries to back them up in every way. And we need them. The eye cannot say to the hand "I have no need of you" (see 1 Cor. 12:21).

The heartbeat of each one of the contributors to this book is that the world may believe; that multitudes of lost men and women will be liberated from the dark oppression of the enemy and drawn by the Holy Spirit to the glorious light of the gospel of Christ. We join Jesus in praying that the Body of Christ will be one in the Spirit.

PRAYING FOR SPIRITUAL UNITY

We are familiar in dealing with public evangelists and cross-cultural missionaries. But can we also apply the same principles and procedures in dealing with spiritual warfare? God will call some to go out to the frontlines and others to do other things. Those who go should not think they are more spiritual or more favored of God than those who do not go. Those who stay at home should not criticize those whom God calls to battle. There should be mutual affirmation and support of all kinds. King David said, "As his part is who goes down to the battle, so shall his part be who stays by the supplies; they shall share alike" (1 Sam. 30:24). When the battle is won, all benefit from the victory—those who went to the frontlines and those who stayed home with their stuff.

I stress this point because I think Satan would like nothing better than to use this book to bring division to the Body of Christ. Jesus prayed to the Father, "That they all may be one...that the world may believe" (see John 17:21). The heart-beat of each one of the contributors to this book is that the world may believe; that multitudes of lost men and women will be liberated from the dark oppression of the enemy and drawn by the Holy Spirit to the glorious light of the gospel of Christ. In order to see this happen we join Jesus in praying that the Body of Christ will be one in the Spirit.

KEEPING THE FOCUS

I know from experience that the subject of spiritual mapping can be so fascinating some fall into the trap of seeing it as an end in itself. Or, perhaps worse yet, some will think we can no longer do evangelism, relief and development or other kinds of ministry without spiritual mapping.

Spiritual mapping is neither an end in itself or an indispensable prerequisite for ministry. It should be seen as just another tool for our task of world evangelization. Examples of dramatic breakthroughs abound in dark places such as Nepal, Algeria or Mongolia without the help of spiritual mapping. However, in those circumstances where spiritual mapping is possible, and when it is done under the anointing of the Holy Spirit, the potential is there for unprecedented forward advances of the Kingdom of God.

My plea is that as you read this book you will keep the focus. The ultimate focus is the glory of God through Jesus Christ who is the King of kings and Lord of lords. Our task is to contribute to that glory spreading through every nation, tribe, tongue and people on the face of the earth.

Notes
1. George Otis, Jr., in a descriptive document introducing "Operation Second Chance," 1992, n.p.
2. Ibid.
3. Samuel Noah Kramer, *From the Tablets of Sumer* (Indian Hills, CO: The Falcon's Wing Press, 1956), p. 271.
4. Ibid., pp. 272,273.
5. Ibid., p. 272.
6. W. F. Kumuyi, *The Key to Revival and Church Growth* (Lagos, Nigeria: Zoe Publishing Company, 1988), p. 25.

Part I:
The Principles

An Overview of Spiritual Mapping

by George Otis, Jr.

GEORGE OTIS, JR. IS FOUNDER AND PRESIDENT OF THE SEN-
tinel Group, organizing global prayer harvest and
high-level spiritual mapping. A former missionary
with YWAM (Youth With a Mission), he also served for
many years as an associate with the Lausanne Commit-
tee for World Evangelization. Currently, George is co-
coordinator, along with Peter Wagner, of the A.D. 2000
Movement United Prayer Track where he heads the Spiritual Mapping division. His book The Last of the Giants
(Chosen) has been widely acclaimed as a bold pioneering effort in the field of spiritual mapping.

In December 1992, I encountered a significant personal milestone—the twentieth anniversary of my involvement in frontier missions. As with all delineating events, the occasion provided cause for both celebration and reflection. It was a time of rejoic-

The Church is presently faced with two substantial external challenges to its continued expansion: "demonic entrenchment" and "the lateness of the hour."

ing in God's faithfulness, but also for contemplating just how radically the world, and the mission field, had changed during these two incredible decades.

Evangelistic progress since the early 1970s has been nothing short of astounding. In addition to major moves of God in Argentina, Russia, Indonesia, Guatemala, Brazil, Nigeria, India, China, South Korea and the Philippines, noteworthy developments have also occurred in such unlikely places as Afghanistan, Nepal, Iran, Mongolia and Saudi Arabia. Successful church planting in the Pacific, Africa and Latin America has largely reduced the world's prime evangelistic real estate to a swath of territory from 10 degree to 40 degree north latitude, running through Northern Africa and Asia known as the "10/40 Window."

A 100 NATION JOURNEY

Over the past 20 years I have had the privilege of viewing much of this evangelistic process on an up-close-and-personal basis. Leadership roles with several missions and movements have afforded me the opportunity of traveling and ministering in nearly 100 nations of the world—a journey that has led me through KGB detention centers, the mean and bloody streets of Beirut, and demon-infested Himalayan monasteries.

This intimate and far-ranging journey has also led me to conclude that the evangelistic progress of recent decades is not likely to be sustained in the future unless Christians become better acquainted with the principles of spiritual warfare. For while the remaining task of world evangelization may be getting smaller (at least insofar as territorial and people group statistics are concerned), it is also becoming more challenging. In the last few years, intercessors and evangelists arrayed on the windowsill of the 10/40 region have found themselves eyeball-to-eyeball with some of the most formidable spiritual strongholds on earth.

The Church is presently faced with two substantial external challenges to its continued expansion: "demonic entrenchment" and "the lateness of the hour."

Although demonic entrenchment is hardly unique—the Hebrews encountered it in both Egypt and Babylon, and the apostle Paul found it in Ephesus—we must consider that we are now centuries deeper into history. In some places on earth today, notably Asia, demonic pacts have been serviced continually since post-deluvian times and spiritual light is nearly imperceptible.

In addition, we must also consider the hour in which we are living. In the book of Revelation, God warns the inhabitants of the earth and the sea, "The devil has come down to you, having great wrath, because he knows that he has a short time" (Rev. 12:12). Increasing reports of gospel incursions into his prayer-eroded strongholds has the enemy realizing that the hour he has long feared is now upon him. Evidence of this is provided in the increasing incidence of demonic signs and wonders, as well as by the stepped-up counterattacks against those who are endeavoring to probe or escape his lair.

In short, Christian warriors at the end of the twentieth century can expect to face challenges on the spiritual battlefield that are unique in both type and magnitude. Commonplace methods of discerning and responding to these challenges will no longer do. As I wrote in my recent book, *The Last of the Giants* (Chosen Books), if we are to successfully overcome the works of the enemy, "We must learn to see the world as it really is, not as it appears to be."

DEFINITIONS AND ASSUMPTIONS

In 1990, I coined a term for this new way of seeing—"spiritual mapping"—now the central theme of this book. It involves, as I have suggested, "Superimposing our understanding of forces and events in the spiritual domain onto places and circumstances in the material world."[1]

The key assumption here is that those who practice spiritual mapping already possess a keen understanding of the spiritual domain. Given the amount of time many Christians spend talking, singing and reading about this dimension in which reality is said to be rooted, it seems as if it should be a reasonable assumption. Unfortunately, it is not. And this is the great surprise.

One would think the ways of the spiritual dimension would be as familiar to the average believer as the sea is to mariners; that the majority of Christians would know in both theory and practice what the apostle Paul was talking about in Ephesians 6 when he spoke of the battle being waged against spiritual hosts of wickedness in the heavenly places.

The problem seems to be that many believers—particularly in the busy Western hemisphere—have not taken the time to learn the language, principles and protocols of the spiritual dimension. Some choose to ignore all but its most cosmic features (heaven, hell, God, the devil), while others tend to project features out of their own imaginations. Both of these tendencies are serious errors. Whereas the former ignores what *is* there, the latter is entranced by what is *not* there. In both cases the works of the devil remain cloaked and the kingdom of darkness flourishes.

Spiritual mapping is a means whereby we can see what is beneath the surface of the material world; but it is not magic. It is subjective in that it is a skill born out of a right relationship with God and a love for His world. It is objective in that it can be verified (or discredited) by history, sociological observation and God's Word.

Nor is spiritual mapping confined solely to the works of darkness. Some spiritual warfare practitioners have given the discipline a narrower definition—limiting it to the discovery of demonic strongholds—but this carries some danger. More specifically, it can encourage a preoccupation with the location and activities of the enemy while ignoring the fact that God also operates in the spiritual dimension. When we superimpose our understanding of forces and events in the spiritual domain onto places and circumstances in the material world, we must remember that these forces and events are not all dark. Spiritual mapping simply puts the works of the enemy into the larger context of the spiritual dimension.

TODAY'S SPIRITUAL BATTLEFIELD

The Church of Jesus Christ must not shrink back from taking a long, hard look at the spiritual obstacles that stand between it and fulfillment of the Great Commission. The spiritual battlefield of the 1990s is increasingly becoming a supernatural place. There are those whose personal theology is resistant to this idea, but these are often untraveled western theoreticians who have yet to put their assumptions to the test of reality. By contrast, the vast majority of today's international pastors, missionaries, evangelists and intercessors have no need to be convinced that something is out there, and this "something" is manifesting itself in our material world.

But what exactly is it that people are noticing? Based on the feedback I have been getting from concerned believers around the world, here are three primary observations:

1. Spiritual darkness is increasing and is becoming more sophisticated.
2. There is a geographical pattern to evil and spiritual oppression.
3. They do not understand the spiritual dimension as well as they thought.

Local churches are discovering that church growth demographics do not tell us everything about our communities. Mission agencies are realizing that cross-cultural savvy alone cannot achieve evangelistic breakthroughs. Intercessory prayer fellowships are acknowledging the need for more specific targeting coordinates. In short, people want answers to the riddle of the invisible world so they can minister more effectively.

TERRITORIAL STRONGHOLDS

Nested near the heart of spiritual mapping philosophy is the concept of territorial strongholds. It is not a new idea; many writers have touched on the theme before. What *is* new is that a growing percentage of the Body of Christ now recognizes the need to deal with such strongholds.

The problem is that the term "territorial strongholds" has been bandied about so freely of late that it begs for definition. Its usage has become so elastic that those who are newly approaching the subject can hardly decide what to believe.

In the confusion, some Christian writers have suggested that any notion of spiritual warfare that embraces spiritual territoriality is extrabiblical. Others have cast doubt on the validity of spiritual warfare itself. Although these voices are clearly in the minority, it is clear that a tightening-up of definitions and usage is in order.

Those who are frightened away from spiritual territoriality by claims that the concept is extrabiblical should remember there is an ocean of difference between that which is "extrabiblical" and that which is "unbiblical." Extrabiblical is a yellow light that encourages passage with caution; unbiblical is a red light that requires travelers to halt in the name of the law and common sense. To date, I have heard no one claim that spiritual territoriality is *unbiblical*. The simple reason for this is that it is not.

Peter Wagner and others have pointed out in earlier writings that the Bible touches on the subject of spiritual territoriality in both Testaments.[2] The most cited instance is the prince of Persia in Daniel 10. Here we have a well-defined case of an evil spiritual being ruling over an area with explicitly proscribed boundaries. Even nonscholars must regard it as significant that this creature is not referred to as the prince of China or the prince of Egypt. When this passage is studied in tandem with verses such as Ezekiel 28:12-19; Deuteronomy 32:8, *Septuagint:* "according to the number of the angels of God"; and Ephesians 6:12, (e.g., *kosmokratoras* "world rulers") the case for spiritual territoriality becomes even more compelling.

As anyone who has paid more than a casual visit to places such as India, Navajoland, Cameroon, Haiti, Japan, Morocco, Peru, Nepal, New Guinea and China will attest, elaborate hierarchies of deities and spirits are regarded as commonplace. These incorporeal beings are perceived to rule over homes, villages, cities, valleys, provinces and nations, and they exercise extraordinary power over the behavior of local peoples. That

God Himself recognized the vicarious power of regional deities is manifest in His urgent calling of Abraham, and later the Hebrew nation, out from amongst the animated pantheons of the Babylonians and Canaanites.

WHY ARE THINGS THE WAY THEY ARE?

Almost everyone has had the experience of entering another city, neighborhood or country only to sense an intangible unease or oppression descend upon their spirits. In many cases, what we are encountering in such circumstances is the prevailing atmosphere of another kingdom. Unbeknownst to us, we have crossed a spiritual boundary that is part of the realm the apostle Paul talks about in Ephesians 6.

Other situations are more obvious. Regardless of their theology, any honest and moderately traveled Christian will acknowledge that there are certain areas of the world today where spiritual darkness is more pronounced. Whether it is the idol-encrusted cities of Varanasi and Kathmandu, the flaunted decadence of Pattaya and Amsterdam, or the spiritual wastelands of Oman and the Western Sahara, in such places reality triumphs over theory every time.

The question is why? Why are some areas more oppressive, more idolatrous, more spiritually barren than others? Why does darkness seem to linger where it does?

Once one begins to ask these primal questions, it is easy to append them to hundreds, even thousands, of specific situations. Why, for instance, has Mesopotamia put out such a long string of tyrannical rulers? Why is the nation of Haiti the premier social and economic eyesore in the Western hemisphere? Why do the Andean nations of South America always seem to rank near the top of the world's annual per capita homicide statistics? Why is there so much overt demonic activity in and around the Himalayan mountains? Why has Japan been such a hard nut to crack with the gospel? Why does the continent of Asia so dominate the 10/40 Window?

Every local church can come up with dozens of other questions right in their own communities. They are not hard to come by, once we consider that it might be relevant to ask such things.

Over the past several years my search for the answers to these questions has taken me literally around the world. It has been a fascinating and instructive journey that has wound through nearly 50 countries and produced more than 35,000 pages of documentary material—including photographs, books, maps, interviews and case studies.

Along the way, I have visited shrines, temples, monasteries, libraries and universities. I have climbed sacred mountains, examined ancestral graveyards, and paddled down the holy Ganges River at dawn. I have listened to the stories of Tibetan Buddhist lamas, native American medicine men and the leading theorists of the New Age movement. I have compared notes with missionaries and frontline national pastors; I have interviewed anthropologists and prehistorians; and I have picked the minds of experts on everything from shamanism and Japanese ancestor worship to folk Islam, geomancy and religious pilgrimages.

The summation of this process, a book and tape series entitled *The Twilight Labyrinth*,[3] is the natural follow-up to *The Last of the Giants* and the book you are now holding in your hands. For those who are serious about identifying and eroding the power of territorial strongholds, this work offers the most comprehensive intelligence to date.

THE RESEARCH CHALLENGE

Those who have read our books know that Peter Wagner and I fully agree that spiritual territoriality has a great deal to do with things being the way they are in certain cities, nations and regions of the world today. Many others—including praying pastors, priests, missionary practitioners and theology professors—have reached a similar conclusion. As encouraging as this growing consensus is, however, many other questions and tasks remain to be addressed.

It is helpful to think of this process in terms of the medical researcher who has just identified a certain virus as the causative agent behind a particular disease. He or she has made an important discovery, but much hard work is ahead if this knowledge is to be translated into practical help for those who are suffering from, or endeavoring to treat, the ailment in question.

The first step is usually to try and come up with some type of diagnostic tool that will help doctors and patients know what they are dealing with at the earliest possible stage. This is helpful in avoiding wild goose chases where treatment is concerned. Misdiagnoses and phantom ailments are both expensive and dangerous.

The next step for researchers is to direct their knowledge of the inner workings of a disease toward an eventual cure. Knowing what causes a problem and how to detect it can ultimately become a heavy burden if this knowledge is not a precursor to resolution.

Acknowledging the role of spiritual territoriality, therefore, is only the departure point for any quest to understand the whys and wherefores of the modern spiritual battlefield. Other probing questions remain. How, for example, are spiritual strongholds established? How are they maintained over time? How are they reproduced in other areas?

Although it is not possible in this brief chapter to answer each of these questions in detail, we can at least cover the basics. In so doing, our starting point is a simple, but crucial, definition. What exactly is a spiritual stronghold? Without delving into the application of the term to mind and imagination, a studied observation of the territorial variety reveals two universal characteristics: they "repel light" and they "export darkness." (Cindy Jacobs describes several kinds of strongholds in chapter 3, but here I am dealing with the territorial kind.)

Territorial strongholds are inherently defensive *and* offensive in nature. While their dark ramparts ward off divine arrows of truth, demonic archers are busy launching fiery darts in the direction of unprotected targets abroad. While their spiritual prison camps retain thousands of enchanted captives, evil command and control centers are releasing manifold deceptions through the spiritual hosts of wickedness in their employ.

ESTABLISHING TERRITORIAL STRONGHOLDS

If we are to understand why things are the way they are today, we must first examine what happened yesterday. Concluding that territorial strongholds exist is not enough. We must also solve the riddle of their origin. Where did they come from? How were they established?

The obvious starting point for this study is at Babel. For as Genesis 11 informs us, it was from the plain of Shinar in ancient Mesopotamia that a geographically coherent people were dispersed by God into the four corners of the earth. But what happened to these ancient peoples as they migrated from Babel? Do ancient artifacts and oral traditions offer us any clues? And, if so, will these clues have any relevance to our quest to understand the origins of territorial strongholds?

Before proceeding further, I should point out one additional fact that bears upon our discussion. Put simply, demons are found wherever there are people. There is no reason for them to be anywhere else. We find no evidence in either Scripture or history that they are interested in inanimate or nonmoral creation, such as mountains, rivers, trees, caves, stars and animals, unless and until people are there. Their bitter mandate is to steal, kill and destroy that which is precious to God; and clearly, human beings created in the divine image are at the top of heaven's list of valuables.

This is the underlying explanation for the darkness that seems to engulf so many of the world's cities. Wherever people congregate in force, demons will be attracted to the scent. Was this not why Babel prompted such swift intervention by God? Is it hard to imagine that the unique concentration of humanity in Shinar would have precipitated the most profound ingathering of demonic powers in history?

Although little is known about the original movements of the first people groups out from Mesopotamia, what we do know suggests at least one experiential common denominator—traumas. For some, it was the inability to traverse forbidding mountain ramparts that blocked their paths. For others, it was a sudden lack of sustenance brought about by severe climatic conditions. Still others found themselves engaged in mortal combat.

Whatever these ancient traumas might have been, they always had the effect of bringing people face-to-face with their desperation. How would they resolve their challenge? Each case was loaded with moral implications. Each circumstance was an opportunity for a specific people in a specific place to return to God in repentance, thereby establishing Him as their rightful ruler and sole deliverer.

Unfortunately, the sackcloth prostrations of Nineveh have proven to be a rare exception to the rule. The overwhelming majority of peoples down through history have elected to exchange the revelations of God for a lie. Heeding the entreaties of demons, they have chosen in their desperation to enter into *quid pro quo* pacts with the spirit world. In return for a particular deity's consent to resolve their immediate traumas, they have offered up their singular and ongoing allegiance. They have collectively sold their proverbial souls.

It is through the placement of these ancient welcome mats, then, that demonic territorial strongholds are established. The basis of the transaction is entirely moral. People make a conscious choice to suppress truth and believe a falsehood. In the end, they are deceived because they choose to be. Peter Wagner eloquently elaborates this in the next chapter by exegeting Romans 1:18-25.

Because many of the oldest pacts between peoples and demonic powers were transacted in Asia, and Asia now hosts the planet's greatest population centers, it should not surprise us that the continent presently dominates the great unreached frontier known as the 10/40 Window. Population and pact longevity both have a great deal to do with the territorial entrenchment of spiritual darkness.

MAINTAINING TERRITORIAL STRONGHOLDS

That dynasties of darkness exist is a sad fact of history. The question that plagues many people is what sustains them. If the misplaced choices of earlier generations allowed demonic forces into certain neighborhoods, how do these evil powers maintain their tenancy rights across centuries or millennia? Put another way, how do they manage lease extensions once those people who signed the original paperwork have passed on?

One major answer to this question is found in the authority transfers that occur during religious festivals, ceremonials and pilgrimages. I have written extensively on this subject in *The Twilight Labyrinth*, and a chronological guide to these events published by our ministry, The Sentinel Group, serves as a counterwarfare handbook for intercessors.

That spiritual power truly is released during these activities has been testified to by numerous national believers and missionaries whom I have interviewed.[4] Nearly all of them speak of a heightened sense of oppression, increased incidents of persecution, and on occasion, wholesale manifestations of demonic signs and wonders. These are difficult times, and the Christians I have talked to are always glad when these incidents are over. Only prayer and praise seems to help, and even then, they sometimes wonder if answers to their prayers are not interrupted by the same kind of spiritual strongman that delayed God's response to Daniel (see Dan. 10:12,13).

It should be noted that religious festivals, ceremonials and pilgrimages are taking place somewhere in the world every week of the year. Literally thousands of these events take place, ranging from localized celebrations to regional and international affairs. Halloween and the Islamic Hajj are well recognized international examples; lesser known regional festivals such as Kumbha Mela in India, Inti Raymi in Peru, and the summer Bon celebrations in Japan, attract huge numbers of participants as well.

Dusting off Ancient Welcome Mats

These celebrations are decidedly not the benign, quaint and colorful cultural spectacles they are often made out to be. They are conscious transactions with the spirit world. They are opportunities for contemporary generations to reaffirm the choices and pacts made by their forefathers and ancestors. They are occasions to dust off ancient welcome mats and extend the devil's right to rule over specific peoples and places today. The significance of these events should not be underestimated.

Once a people have given in to vain imaginations, demonic powers are quick to animate resulting mythologies. In a manner reminiscent of the Wizard of Oz, manipulative spiritual agents practice the art of shadow-ruling from behind the scenes. The authority and allegiance rendered to so-called protective deities is quickly absorbed—and from that moment on, the lie is enchanted.

Unfortunately, hundreds of thousands of children a day are

born into these enchanted systems around the world. Nearly all of them grow up hearing about the lie, but it is during the course of puberty rites and initiations that many of them feel its intense gravitational suction for the first time. The power of the lie, fueled by demonic magic, is called tradition; and it is tradition, in turn, that sustains territorial dynasties.

Adaptive Deception

As important as tradition is in maintaining territorial dynasties, however, it is not the *only* means the enemy uses to accomplish this end. Another equally important strategy is what I call "adaptive deception." It is employed when tradition, for whatever reason, begins to lose its potency in a given society.

Adaptive deceptions are, depending on how one chooses to view them, either necessary course corrections, or upgrades to the devil's "product line." They work because of humankind's propensity to try new things. Put more crudely, and with apologies to feline aficionados, the devil has learned that there is more than one way to skin a cat.

Two modern-day examples of adaptive deceptions are found in folk Islam and Japanese New Religions. Folk Islam is a combination of animist and Islamic beliefs, and many of the Japanese New Religions present a curious synthesis of Buddhist and materialistic concepts. In terms of numbers of adherents or practitioners, both are hugely successful.

Adaptive deceptions do not *replace* preexisting ideological bondages, they *augment* them. In this sense, they are analogous on a collective level to the biblical account of the demon that returns to the undefended human vessel with seven other spirits more wicked than itself (Matt. 12:43-45; Luke 11:24-26).

PREVAILING BONDAGES AND ROOT BONDAGES

Now that we are armed with an understanding of the roles that adaptive deception, tradition and religious festivals play in maintaining territorial dynasties, we must learn one final lesson. It has to do with discerning the difference between "prevailing bondages" and "root bondages." Due to a lack of teaching on this subject, Christian warriors are often misled by surface appearances when they endeavor to identify territorial strongholds.

A good example of this was raised by the large number of people who insisted a few years ago that the spiritual stronghold over Albania was Stalinist communism. Although there is no doubt that communism was the *prevailing* bondage at the time, it was also widely assumed to be the root stronghold. The flaw in this reasoning becomes obvious when one considers that communism did not become the predominant ideology in the country until 1944. The significance of this fact is, that as vile and destructive as this atheistic system was, it was only in place for some 50 years. Albanian history, meanwhile, goes back to biblical Illyricum and is many thousands of years old.

Similar Johnny-come-lately systems can be found in Mesopotamia, Japan and other areas of the world. They represent topsoil ideologies that come and go with the wind. Although they cannot be ignored, neither should they be mistaken for the spiritual bedrock that must be broken up if we are to entertain legitimate hopes of seeing territorial strongholds successfully invaded with the gospel.

THE EXPANSION OF DARKNESS

Having looked at the questions of how spiritual strongholds are established and maintained, we turn now to the subject of territorial expansion. Here we are interested in knowing if the kingdom of darkness is geographically dynamic, and if it is, how the characteristics of certain strongholds are reproduced in other areas.

In *The Twilight Labyrinth* I have devoted an entire chapter to territorial dynamics entitled "The Banyan Way." As the title suggests, I have seized upon the tropical banyan tree, with its extending branches and descending aerial roots, as an excellent analogy of the way the kingdom of darkness expands.

Starting from a single massive trunk, the banyan's sinuous branches extend laterally in all directions. From these, in what is surely the tree's most remarkable feature, aerial roots descend to the ground to form new trunks. In this fashion, the banyan can move laterally over great distances—creating as it does, an often impenetrable thicket of twisting, vine-like branches and trunks.

These extending branches and descending roots represent the two ways territorial expansion takes place: "ideological export" and "trauma-induced strongholds." Ideological export, a lateral extension of territorial strongholds, is accomplished through the broadcast of ideological or spiritual influence from transmission sites, or export centers, in various areas of the world. Examples of such centers include Cairo, Tripoli, Karbala, Qom and Mecca in the Muslim world; Allahabad and Varanasi in the Hindu world; Dharamsala and Tokyo in the Buddhist world; and Amsterdam, New York, Paris and Hollywood in the materialistic world. Whereas the deflector shields of Judeo-Christian values once kept such poison from seeping too deeply into North America, the erosion of Christian commitment in recent years has unfortunately come to mean that, in an increasing number of instances, the enemy is now us.

Another way the enemy expands his kingdom in the world is by inducing new traumas. Having learned from past experience how effectively desperate circumstances can draw men and women into his web, he will often use the greed, lust and dishonesty of depraved individuals to create fresh crises.

One graphic example of a trauma-induced stronghold in the Western hemisphere is Haiti. Taking advantage of the greed of Efik tribesmen and French slave traders, huge numbers of West Africans were brought to the Caribbean and mistreated to the point of desperation. Choosing to resolve their conflict by entering into fresh pacts with the spirit world, these slaves established an animist-based system of worship and secret rule known as voudon. Today, the dark rewards of this system are

---

Could it be that it is God's plan for His Church to complete the Great Commission on the very selfsame soil where the original commandment was delivered to earth's first family?

---

widely known, as Peter Wagner goes on to show in the following chapter.

THE THRESHOLD GENERATION

As the armies of the Lord Jesus Christ begin to collapse the remaining task of world evangelization on the 10/40 Window, it is curious that the geographic centerpoint of this region should be the site of ancient Eden (i.e. in the area of Iraq, also see Gen. 2:8-14). Could it be that it is God's plan for His Church to complete the Great Commission on the very selfsame soil where the original commandment was delivered to earth's first family? (See Genesis 1:27,28.)

Whatever the answer, it is clear that Christian warriors who dare to march this final road will face formidable opposition from an implacable and invisible adversary. If their mission to liberate enchanted prisoners is to succeed, they will require accurate intelligence on enemy command and control centers, and the spiritual equivalent of the military's night vision goggles.

It is impossible to unpack three years worth of spiritual mapping intelligence in one chapter. Nevertheless, it is my hope that this information will at least alert those readers who are contemplating imminent rescue missions to the fact that new tools are becoming available to guide them through the twists and turns of the twilight labyrinth.

▰ REFLECTION QUESTIONS ▰

1. Discuss the concept of "spiritual territoriality." Do you agree that spiritual principalities of evil could have been assigned by Satan to certain geographic regions?
2. This chapter suggests that religious festivals can reinforce the authority of evil powers over an area. Name and discuss as many of these festivals as you can think of.
3. Have you ever experienced an almost physical sensation of darkness and oppression in a certain area of your city or nation? Share your feelings with others.
4. Demonic strongholds over a city or nation can be induced by traumas. Can you think of any such traumas in the history of your city or nation that might have produced strongholds?
5. Review George Otis, Jr.'s distinction between concepts that are "extrabiblical" and "unbiblical." Do you agree?

Notes

1. George Otis, Jr., *The Last of the Giants* (Tarrytown, NY: Chosen Books, 1991), p. 85.
2. See, for example, C. Peter Wagner, *Warfare Prayer* (Ventura, CA: Regal Books, 1992), pp. 87-103.
3. Additional information on these and other intercessory support products is available through: The Sentinel Group, P.O. Box 6334, Lynnwood, WA 98036.
4. Specific testimonies have been gathered in Japan, Morocco, Indonesia, Haiti, India, Bhutan, Egypt, Turkey, Nepal, Afghanistan, Iran, Fiji, American Indian reservations and elsewhere.

The Visible and the Invisible

by C. Peter Wagner

N ATTEMPT TO SEE THE WORLD AROUND US AS IT REALLY IS, not as it appears to be. This is the classic description of spiritual mapping.

An important assumption behind spiritual mapping is that reality is more than appears on the surface. The visible things of our daily life—trees, people, cities, stars, governments, animals, professions, art, behavior patterns—are commonplace and taken for granted. However, behind many visible aspects of the world around us may be spiritual forces, invisible areas of reality that may have more ultimate significance than the visible.

The apostle Paul hints strongly at this when he says, "We do not look at the things which are seen, but at the things which are not seen. For the things which are seen are temporary, but the things which are not seen are eternal" (2 Cor. 4:18).

Paul says that recognizing the difference between the visible and the invisible will keep us from "losing heart" (see 2 Cor. 4:16). Losing heart over what? He mentions losing heart once again in the first verse of the chapter, and then laments that his evangelistic efforts are not all that he wished them to be. "Our gospel is veiled...to those who are perishing," he writes. Why? Because the "god of this age" has blinded their minds (see 2 Cor. 4:3,4).

I understand Paul's message to mean we must recognize that the essential battle for world evangelization is a spiritual battle and that the weapons of this warfare are not carnal but spiritual. We must also recognize that God has given us a mandate for intelligent, aggressive spiritual warfare. If we understand this, the more the process of world evangelization will be accelerated. Understanding the differences between the visible and the invisible is one important component of the overall battle plan to break the hold the enemy has on lost and perishing souls.

Igniting the Wrath of God

The key biblical passage on distinguishing the visible from the invisible, Romans 1, is also a passage on the wrath of God. Understandably, the wrath of God is not one of our favorite subjects so we do not have many books on it or hear many sermons on it. Nevertheless, wrath is an attribute of God. This means it is not just some mood that comes and goes, but a part of the very nature of God. God is a God of wrath. He is also a God of justice, a God of love, a God of mercy and a God of holiness. The list could go on. But Romans 1:18-31 deals with the God of *wrath*.

Paul says, "The wrath of God is revealed from heaven against all ungodliness and unrighteousness of men, who suppress the truth in unrighteousness" (Rom. 1:18). This madden-

---

God created the world to manifest His glory. Every human being was created to glorify God. Humans occupy a higher level than other objects of creation because we are the only ones created in the image of God.

---

ing unrighteousness has directly to do with the visible and the invisible. Let me explain.

Why did God create the world? He created the world to manifest His glory. Paul explains that through "the things that are made," or the visible aspects of creation, God's "invisible attributes are clearly seen." Everything we see in God's creation, without exception, was originally created to reveal "His eternal power and Godhead." (See Rom. 1:19,20.)

What does this mean for us? It means, for a starter, that every human being was created to glorify God. Humans occupy a higher level than other objects of creation because we are the only ones created in the image of God. Every angelic being was also created to glorify God. So was every animal, all plants, heavenly bodies, mountains, icebergs, volcanoes and uranium, just to name a few. Human culture is also a part of God's creation, designed to glorify Him. I will deal with this one in some detail as the chapter progresses.

CORRUPTING GOD'S CREATION

The fact of the matter is that in our world not all parts of creation do glorify God. Certain human beings have taken created things and corrupted them so that they no longer reveal God's glory. They have changed God's glory "into an image made like corruptible man—and birds and four-footed beasts and creeping things" (Rom. 1:23). God is literally infuriated when He sees what was designed for His glory being switched to, specifically, humans, birds, animals and reptiles. When such visible objects are intentionally crafted to represent supernatural powers, they release the wrath of God.

If we trace references to the wrath of God through the Bible, it is clear that nothing even comes close to upsetting God as much as "serving the creature rather than the Creator" (see Rom. 1:25). God especially hates it when human beings use the visible to glorify Satan and other evil demonic beings. Just reading Jeremiah chapters 1-19 will strike fear in the heart of anyone who would dare to do such a horrible thing, as the people of Judah were bent on doing despite Jeremiah's warnings. They were "Saying to a tree 'You are my father,' and to a stone, 'You gave birth to me'" (Jer. 2:27). This hurts God so much that He looks upon it as adultery: "You have played the harlot with many lovers" (Jer. 3:1). He said, "[Israel] defiled the land and committed adultery with stones and trees" (Jer. 3:9).

I do not think the order of the Ten Commandments is a mere happenstance. God hates murder, stealing, immorality, violating the Sabbath and covetousness. But all of those come after commandments number one and number two: "You shall have no other gods before Me" and "You shall not make for yourself any carved image" (Exod. 20:3,4). The first commandment has to do with the invisible and the second commandment with the visible.

I think it is safe to say that no sin is worse than using the visible to give honor and glory to demonic principalities. Nothing so provokes God to jealousy and wrath.

Japan and the Rising Sun

Japan, for example, is known as the "land of the rising sun." The sun, of course, is a feature of God's creation designed to glorify Him. Japan's flag pictures nothing but the sun. It is the symbol of the nation. But does the sun on Japan's flag glorify God? No. It is used with the intentional purpose of glorifying *Amaterasu Omikami*, the sun-goddess who is a recognized and enshrined territorial spirit ruling Japan.

People should look at the Japanese flag and say, "Praise God!" Instead they use it to glorify the creature rather than the Creator.

Hawaiian Lava Rock

When I recently did a spiritual warfare conference in Hawaii, I found that many people were focused on rocks, especially lava rocks formed by the Kiluea volcano. They should look at those beautiful lava rocks and say, "Glory to God! Our God is a consuming fire." He is their Creator.

But, no. Many Hawaiian people look at the rocks and say, "Glory to Pele! If we don't honor her, she will consume us with fire." God's attitude? According to Romans 1, it makes Him very angry.

The Grand Canyon

Most American Christians would agree that for natural features, the Grand Canyon is unsurpassed as a visible manifestation of the majesty of God. Few of them, however, would recognize, as did David and Jane Rumph, that some person or persons have systematically corrupted it and made it a monument of geographical idolatry. In a recent article, they said that "righteous rage" welled up in them as they began seeing the perverse invisible forces now glorified by the visible natural features. Regrettably, the vast majority of Grand Canyon features carry the names of principalities and powers of darkness.

Some glorify Egyptian spirits: Tower of Ra, Cheops Pyramid, Osiris Temple; some glorify Hindu principalities: Vishnu Creek, Rama Shrine, Krishna Shrine; Greek and Roman deities: Jupiter Temple, Juno Temple, Venus Temple, just to take a random sampling. Add to that Phantom Creek, Haunted Canyon and Crystal Dragon Creek and you have a sure formula for provoking God's wrath.

I like the Rumphs's response. They suggest we should, "In humility repent on behalf of our people for this corporate sin, declare that that place rightfully belongs to God, and intercede for the Lord to be honored there through new names."[1]

Affirming Culture

We live in a time worldwide, and particularly in the United States, when a new respect for culture is developing. It is becoming fashionable to reaffirm culture and to advocate a multicultural society. This must not be allowed to blindside Christians. We need to understand it in the light of the visible and the invisible. Behind cultural forms, just as behind lava rock in Hawaii, can lie the invisible power of the Creator or invisible demonic power. If we are ignorant of this, we can make ourselves unnecessarily vulnerable to devastating waves of high-level demonization.

Human culture, as I have mentioned, is a part of God's creation. Therefore, culture in and of itself is good. It is one of the visible elements designed to glorify the Creator. This is such a crucial point that I want to reinforce it by making reference both to the Old Testament and to the New Testament.

The Tower of Babel

Cultural origins are revealed in Genesis. There was a time, according to Genesis 11, when the human race was all one culture. Presumably, however, God's original purpose was to have the human race scatter over the earth and develop into diverse cultures. But the people, true to their fallen nature, thought they had a better plan than God. So they decided to reverse the scattering process by consolidating around a tower, the Tower of Babel. They built the tower explicitly: "Lest we be scattered abroad over the face of the whole earth" (Gen. 11:4).

The tower was a visible structure. What was the invisible? Archaeologists tell us it was a typical ziggurat, a well-known ancient structure designed for occult purposes. They wanted a tower "whose top is in the heavens" in order to draw on satanic power for their desired one world movement. They used the visible to glorify the creature rather than the Creator.

God's reaction was predictable. He became angry. In one stroke He ruined their plans by confounding their languages, and they proceeded to scatter as God had intended. The human race ended up, "Separated into their lands, everyone according to his own language, according to their families, into their nations" (Gen. 10:5).

Biblical scholars are divided on whether today's human cultures are a *punishment* of God (God's Plan B) or a *purpose of God* (God's Plan A). I believe cultures are a part of God's creative purpose, Plan A. At Babel, God did not *change* His long-range plans, He simply *accelerated* them. In my view, what might have taken centuries or millennia happened in an instant.

For one thing, it is not unlike God to produce diversity. Look at the different kinds of butterflies He created. Or fish. Or flowers. The world is a much better world with diversity than without. Diverse cultures fit the pattern.

The Redemptive Gift

Each culture or each people group or each nation makes a contribution no other can make. Many, following John Dawson's pioneering work in *Taking Our Cities for God*, refer to this cultural uniqueness as the "redemptive gift."[2] A crucial part of spir-

---

> Our goal is to restore God's glory to every detail of His creation. Knowing God's redemptive gift provides specific, positive direction to our praying and other activities in spiritual warfare.

---

itual mapping is to identify the redemptive gift or, as some say, redemptive purpose of a city or a nation or other networks of humans. In fact, it is the *most* crucial part. Ultimately, our goal is not to expose satanic strongholds, unmask occultic deception, pursue spiritual mapping or bind principalities and powers. Our goal is to restore God's glory to every detail of His creation. Knowing God's redemptive gift provides specific, positive direction to our praying and other activities in spiritual warfare.

If any questions remain whether human cultures were a part of the intentional purpose of God, they should be resolved by the apostle Paul's remarks on Mars Hill in Athens. There he affirms, "He [God] has made from one blood every nation of men to dwell on all the face of the earth, and has determined their preappointed times and the boundaries of their habitation" (Acts 17:26). And what was God's purpose in making so many different people groups or cultures? "So that they should seek the Lord" (Acts 17:27). It was clearly a redemptive purpose.

The Bad News: Culture Has Been Corrupted

The good news is that cultures are designed to glorify God. The bad news is that for the most part they do not. Satan has succeeded in corrupting them. Satan's chief goal is to prevent God from being glorified. He did it first by provoking the Fall of Adam and Eve and corrupting the very human nature that was created in the image of God. Then, using multitudes of depraved human beings, he has continued his perverse activity on the level of society as a whole.

Paul follows this theme in his sermon on Mars Hill, an entire message on the visible and the invisible. He preached it because, "His spirit was provoked within him when he saw that the city was given over to idols" (Acts 17:16). In this sermon, Paul points out two common cultural forms often used to glorify demonic forces of darkness: temples and art. Athens was full of temples but, "Since He is Lord of heaven and earth, does not dwell in temples made with hands" (Acts 17:24). Athens was known for its art, but, "The Divine Nature is [not] like gold or silver or stone, something shaped by art and man's devising" (Acts 17:29).

Certainly both architecture and art can glorify God, and much does. But they can also be chief instruments of glorifying the creature, Satan and his cohorts, rather than the Creator.

Anthropologists analyze things such as architecture and art as well as human behavior in various cultures. They are able to distinguish, often quite accurately, forms, functions and meanings of cultural components. But even the best social scientists can deal only with the visible. To go beyond that requires a dimension foreign to cultural anthropology—discernment of spirits. Anthropology sees culture *as it appears to be*, while spiritual mapping attempts to see culture *as it really is*.

Early missionaries, who were not grounded in cultural anthropology as today's missionaries are, made a common mistake. When they entered another culture they knew there was an enemy, and they wrongly concluded that the enemy was culture. They did the best they could, but they left behind many things that we all regret now. Today we understand that culture is not the enemy, but Satan is. Our central task is discerning where the *invisible* has corrupted the *visible*, and dealing with it through power encounter (2 Cor. 10:4,5). Our goal is to block Satan's work and bring forth God's redemptive gift, not to destroy culture.

REAFFIRMING CULTURES IN AMERICA

It does not take much discernment of spirits to know that one of the most powerful strongholds the enemy has in American society goes back to slavery and is currently manifested just as strongly in racism. We have sought, and will continue to seek, political ways and means to overcome this societal corruption, but it seems like each step forward produces an equal step backward.

Lincoln's Emancipation Proclamation freeing the slaves in 1863 was a step forward. But then the resulting white supremacy that developed culturally perverse patterns such as "assimilation" (i.e., blacks must become like whites in order to be accepted), or misleading slogans such as "America is a melting pot" (i.e., all Americans are the same) was clearly a step backward. It mixed a good thing, "we should all be color blind" with a bad one, "we're blind to our racism."

It took 100 years, until the Civil Rights Movement of the 1960s began to shed these ideas. We began to realize that black is beautiful and that blacks can be blacks and still be good Americans. We began to reaffirm African-American culture, as well as the cultures of our other American minorities. This was the step forward. The step backward, which is so new that many are not yet aware of it, is a dangerous and somewhat naive opening to paganism. Here is where it relates directly to the visible and the invisible.

Exaggerating Tolerance

Tolerance is the opposite of discrimination. In the effort to reassert cultural pluralism, tolerance becomes a high value. Intolerant groups such as the Ku Klux Klan are considered unfortunate societal deviants today. This is a step forward.

My fear is that when tolerance becomes exaggerated, it might take us *two* steps backward and the end could be worse than the beginning. This is because although the visible forms of culture might be neutral and worthy of tolerance, this is not true of all the invisible spiritual powers behind certain cultural forms. Solomon found this out when he brought women from different cultures into his harem. The women and the art and artifacts they brought from their pagan cultures were one thing. The demonic principalities and powers that came along with them were something else and they eventually led to Solomon's downfall (1 Kings 11:4-10). The invisible came along with the visible.

Good Americans these days are expected to tolerate anything from homosexual life-styles to Eastern religions. Multiculturalism is the byword on campuses. Journalists, artists, teachers and judges must be "politically correct." Notice where this takes us. When tolerance is supreme, the only thing not to be tolerated is intolerance. Christianity, by nature, is seen as intolerant because it claims that God is absolute, that His Word is truth, that His morality is normative, and that only through Jesus Christ can lost human beings regain their personal relationship to Him. Christianity is anything but politically correct.

This is why we cannot pray or read our Bibles or post the Ten Commandments in our public schools. This is why the University of Washington is asking Campus Crusade leaders to sign forms requiring them to open their leadership to all students regardless of religious creed or sexual orientation. Tim Stafford reports, "At Stanford people can say pretty much anything they want about white males or religious fundamentalists, but woe betide the individual who says or does something deemed offensive to the oppressed: women, homosexuals, the disabled, or people of color."[3]

This is bad enough, but more alarming is that these attitudes are creeping into mainstream Christianity. Recent research by George Barna has revealed that only 23 percent of born-again, evangelical Christians believe there is such a thing as absolute truth![4] No wonder some are questioning the need for aggressive evangelism. Maybe faith in Jesus Christ as Lord and Savior is not really that crucial after all!

When seen in the light of the visible and the invisible, this is not a cultural game we are playing. Reinviting paganism into our society under the guise of tolerance furnishes strongholds for territorial spirits to invade and take control. It courts societal demonization and ultimate disaster for the people.

What the Powers of Darkness Do

How dangerous is this? When demonic forces control society many things can happen. We are seeing a few of them develop before our eyes in America. For example:

1. They can provoke a resurgence of racism in new and even more violent forms. Minorities can turn against minorities such as conflicts between African-Americans and Korean-Americans or between Hispanic-Americans and African-Americans.
2. They can divert the legislative and judicial systems into legalizing rights of pressure groups, no matter how damaging their causes might be to society as a whole in the long run. Exaggerated animal rights, gay rights, environmental trivia and abortion for convenience are seen as politically correct.

3. They can open the doors to moral decay. When people worship the creature and not the Creator, morality shipwrecks as Romans 1 reveals in no uncertain
terms. Society can get so bad that God gives up on its
people. Three times in Romans 1, Paul repeats, "God
gave them up." To what? To (1) "the lusts of their
hearts, to dishonor their bodies among themselves"
(1:24); (2) "men with men committing what is shame-
ful" (1:27); (3) "a debased mind, to do those things
which are not fitting" (1:28); and this is followed by
one of the most revolting lists of sinful practices found
in the Bible. Regretfully, every item on that list can be
found on the front pages of our city newspapers in
America today.

THE CHALLENGE OF SPIRITUAL DISCERNMENT

In a national and international environment where cultures are
being affirmed and where tolerance is expected, where do we
draw the line? On the one hand, we want to affirm the culture.
After all, God created each culture and gave it a redemptive
gift or gifts for His glory. On the other hand, we want to
unmask the satanic deceptions that are blocking the emergence
of God's glory. We want to identify the strongholds and, following biblical principles of spiritual warfare, tear them down
and serve eviction notices to the spiritual forces behind them (2
Cor. 10:3-5; Eph. 6:12). The more skillful we become at spiritual mapping, the more effective we will be in meeting such a
challenge.

Sometimes, knowing where to draw the line is relatively
easy. It can be done with spiritual common sense. At other
times, it is a delicate situation requiring spiritual gifts such as
prophecy and discernment of spirits, as well as considerable

field experience. Let me give a personal example and a biblical example of drawing such lines.

Cleansing Wagners' Living Room

Readers of other books in this series will know that my wife, Doris, and I have had to deal with evil spirits in our home in Altadena, California. In one of the books in this series, *Prayer Shield* (Regal Books), I detailed the story of my fall off a ladder in my garage and how I believe that Cathy Schaller's intercession at that time literally saved my life. Evidence points toward attributing it to the direct work of an evil spirit. In another book, *Warfare Prayer* (Regal Books), I told of Doris actually seeing a spirit in our bedroom and of how Cathy Schaller and George Eckart subsequently came to our house and exorcised the spirits.

Cathy and George had found more spirits in our living room than in other rooms. When they left, they felt they had evicted them all except for one, which they discerned was attached to a stone puma from the Quechua Indian culture we had acquired while we were missionaries in Bolivia. The puma was not an antique, just a tourist reproduction, but nevertheless the invisible had apparently attached itself to the visible. Besides the puma, we had as wall decorations two pagan masks used by the Chiquitano Indians, and two carved wooden lamps representing the Aymara Indian culture.

When Doris and I returned home from work that day we had some decisions to make. Where do we draw the line? We had three different sets of art objects from three of Bolivia's Indian cultures.

1. The puma. Believing that an evil spirit had attached itself to the puma, the decision was simple. The puma had to go. We took it outside, smashed it up, and threw it in the garbage.

2. The masks. If Cathy and George's discernment was accurate, no spirits had attached themselves to the masks. However, those masks were not tourist reproductions. They had actually been used by the Chiquitano Indians in their animistic ceremonies designed to glorify their tribal spirits. Even with the little we knew in those days, this seemed to be reason enough to get rid of the masks, which we did.

3. The lamps. The lamps were something else. They were beautiful works of native art. They were carved and varnished reproductions of *Inti*, the sun-god who was one of the territorial spirits over the highland Aymara Indians. They were one of the most expensive items we brought home from Bolivia. They matched our decor perfectly. They were not demonized as the puma was. So we discussed it and decided we should regard them as native art and not as idols or unclean objects. We kept the lamps.

We kept them until the first time Cindy Jacobs visited our home. Cindy, the author of the following chapter on demonic strongholds, was way ahead of Doris and me in her discernment of spirits and knowledge of spiritual mapping. She stepped into our living room, and with a rather shocked look on her face said, "What are those things doing here?" pointing to the lamps. We explained that they were just harmless souvenirs to remind us of our days in Bolivia. Then Cindy said gently, "Well, why don't you pray about them?" and the subject did not come up again.

After Cindy left, we did pray. This time God directed us to take a different approach to our decision. We finally realized we had never asked ourselves the most crucial question: Do these objects glorify God? In the light of what we were by then understanding as the biblical truth on the visible and the invisible, the answer was obviously no. The hands that had made the lamps, skillful as they might have been, "Changed the glory of the incorruptible God into an image made like corruptible man" (Rom. 1:23). The net result was to bring glory to the sun-god, *Inti*, who is the creature, rather than to the Creator. The lamps also had to go!

Later we read Deuteronomy 7:25,26 referring to "carved images of gods," exactly what our *Intis* were. It says they are "abominations to the Lord." And then: "Nor shall you bring an abomination into your house, lest you be doomed to destruction like it; but you shall utterly detest it and utterly abhor it, for it is an accursed thing." We saw clearly how wrong we were in regarding the lamps as harmless native art.

Our house was cleansed. It was only recently that our adult daughter Becky told us that while she was a child growing up in the house, she would never go into the living room alone. She was not able to verbalize it then, but she sensed it was contaminated with dark powers. How ignorant we parents were!

How Paul Drew the Line

It seems the Corinthian Christians were about as ignorant of the visible and the invisible as the Wagners. In their context, the problem arose with meat that had been offered to idols. Paul helps them know where to draw the line in 1 Corinthians 8-10.

We must understand that the visible aspects of this issue, namely idols and meat, are not the chief problem. Paul asks the rhetorical questions: "What am I saying then? That an idol is anything, or what is offered to idols is anything?" (1 Cor. 10:19). The obvious answer is no. The real problem is the invisible demons behind them.

Corinthians could ordinarily secure idol meat in three places: (1) in the public market, (2) in friends' homes on social occasions, and (3) in the idol temple itself. Where should they draw the line?

1. The public market. Go ahead and buy the meat there without asking any questions. (See 1 Cor. 10:25.)

2. Dinner at a friend's home. Eat the meat if no one makes an issue of it. However, if the fact that the meat was offered to idols is announced, do not eat it. (See 1 Cor. 10:27,28.)

3. In the idol temple. Do not do it. Why? Because although the invisible spirits may not be present in the meat itself or in a friend's dining room, they definitely are present in the idol temples. Paul says, "The things which the Gentiles sacrifice they sacrifice to demons." He goes on, "I do not want you to have fellowship with demons" (1 Cor. 10:20).

It is not always easy to know where to draw these lines. But it is always wise to raise three questions whenever there is a doubt:

- Might this open me to direct demonic influence?
- Does this give any appearance of evil?
- Does this glorify God?

Limits of Authority

Drawing the line is one thing. Taking direct action against an object or a behavior is something else. I could destroy the artifacts in my living room because I was the legal owner and thus they were under my authority. Neither Becky nor Cindy could have taken that initiative, much as they might have liked to. In many life situations the presence of visible objects that glorify the creature rather than the Creator is a given and we can do nothing about it.

For example, the building in which Doris and I have our A.D. 2000 United Prayer Track offices features a grossly unclean statue at its entrance. In fact, the finger of that undesirable individual points directly into the window of my office. If I had the authority, I would certainly remove the statue and destroy it. But I do not. So since I cannot deal with the visible, I have dealt with the invisible.

Doris and I invited Cindy Jacobs to join us in an office cleansing when we first moved in. She broke the power of spirits inside the office and bound any forces of darkness attached to the statue. Since then the offices have been peaceful and pleasant. Whether there is yet an invisible power behind the statue I do not know. But I do know we are now protected by having taken authority in the name of Jesus over the part of the building that we lease.

NATIONAL DEMONIZATION

I have attempted to stress that ignoring the reality of invisible powers behind visible aspects of daily life can have serious and even devastating effects both individually and socially. Two nations have recently taken foolish official action on the highest government level to invite demonic principalities to empower their land: Haiti and Japan.

Haiti

Haiti has long been the poorest nation of the Western Hemisphere. Through the years, religion brought by the Roman Catholic Church has not helped. Vigorous Protestant missionary work has not helped. Politics have not helped. Foreign aid has not helped.

Perhaps Haiti's greatest ray of hope for a better future came in December 1990 when Jean-Bertrand Aristide became the first democratically elected president in Haiti's history. On a slate of 11 candidates he received 67 percent of the vote, a relatively unheard of phenomenon in multiparty elections.

Things were looking up. A few months after Aristide's inauguration, Jim Shahim reported, "Haiti seems like a different place." Human rights violations were down. The boat people exodus stopped. Aristide, in a visit to Paris, received promises of $500 million for a variety of projects. People were talking about the new mood. Even one of Aristide's political opponents called him, "Our messiah of hope."[5]

Preserving cultural roots. Then Aristide, whether knowingly or unknowingly, as he is also a Catholic priest, made a
serious spiritual mistake. On August 14, 1991, he officially
requested that Haiti's top voodoo witch doctors lead a national observance of the voodoo ceremony of Boukmann to reded-
icate the nation of Haiti to the spirits of the dead. The ceremony typically involves animal, and some say human, sacrifice.
Why? Purportedly to "preserve Haiti's cultural roots."

A month or so later, on September 29, 1991, Aristide was
ousted by a military coup. Haiti took a socioeconomic nose-
dive. An international embargo was imposed. Normal economy
became virtually nonexistent. Tens of thousands of jobs were
lost, many irrevocably. Months after the coup, Howard W.
French reported, "Port-au-Prince, a bustling city in normal
times, now often seems a dusty ghost town."[6] Public services
were suspended because of lack of gasoline, and garbage was
piled high on the streets. Many foreign investors gave up totally on Haiti. The nation reached the lowest point on the human
misery scale.

What really happened? Political analysts are trained to see
the *visible.* They say Aristide was overthrown by the rich
because he was a liberation theologian and favored the poor.
Or that military officers turned against him because of his
antidrug policies and his desire to form a security unit outside
army control. There are other reasons.

Spiritual mappers, however, see the *invisible.* Although not
negating the validity of the political analysis, they see behind it
the sinister working of spiritual powers using human beings
and social structures such as the military for their own ends.
Not only the voodoo practitioners but the territorial spirits ruling over Haiti were delighted to accept the president's invitation to national demonization. Once they had their legal
strongholds to victimize Haiti's masses by stealing, killing and
destroying, they had no more use for their "friend" Jean-

Bertrand Aristide and they relegated him to the political trash heap. His plan to "reaffirm Haitian culture" backfired because he could not discern the invisible evil from the visible good.

Japan

I once asked David Yonggi Cho why he thought churches grew so rapidly in Korea but not in Japan. His answer surprised me. Although recognizing that there are many reasons, one, he suggested, was the serious damage done to traditional Korean culture through 36 years of Japanese occupation and subsequently through communism from the north. Christianity grew relatively unhindered by traditional Korean paganism.

On the other hand, Japan's culture has been virtually uninterrupted for 3,000 years. Paganism is deeply rooted in the warp and woof of the nation. The spirits over Japan have had their way and they are not prepared to allow Christianity more than a token presence.

The most serious setback for Japan's territorial spirits came during a seven-year period following World War II. Despite a Buddhist facade, Japan's most deeply entrenched spirits undoubtedly are the principalities controlling Shintoism, which is a spiritualized form of nationalism. The chief visible figure employed by these dark angels is the emperor. In the popular mind, the emperor was himself a deity. But as a part of the World War II peace process, he publicly denied this status and the Japanese government agreed to separate itself officially from any religious institution, including Shintoism. General MacArthur called for thousands of Christian missionaries, many went, and Christianity grew well for what are now known as the "seven wonderful years."

For more than 30 years it appeared in the visible that Japan was maintaining its status quo. But in the invisible world the dark angels seemed to be regaining their foothold. The growth of the church slowed to a crawl. Then the emperor died and his son would become the new emperor. A crucial question revolved around the *Daijosi* ceremony, the spiritual component of the traditional inauguration of a new emperor. The *Daijosi*, choreographed through divination and occultic rituals, would climax in a sexual encounter between the new emperor and the sun-goddess, *Amaterasu Omikami*, a chief spiritual ruler over the nation. It matters little whether the ensuing intercourse is physical (succubus) or spiritual. In the *invisible* world the two ritually become one flesh and through its supreme leader the nation invites demonic control.

Unfortunately for Japan, as for Haiti, a foolish decision was made and the new emperor decided to reverse his father's post-World War II position and once again became in the popular mind, "deified" through the *Daijosi* ceremony. Not only that, but the government paid the expenses of the multimillion dollar ritual over the vehement protests of Japanese Christian leaders.

Since then, predictably, the overt participation of government officials, as national leaders, in pilgrimages and rituals connected with traditional Japanese paganism, have been on the increase. What this means for the nation long range remains to be seen. But at this writing the Japanese stock market and its ripple effect on both Japanese and international economies is in its steepest decline since World War II, a decline that dates back to the *Daijosi* ceremony.

How About the United States?

The United States is quite different from Haiti and Japan, both of which have reasonably homogeneous populations. Reaffirming "Haitian cultural roots" or "Japanese traditional culture" has a widely understood meaning. But the United States leads the world in national multiculturalism. In the United States, the reaffirmation could come only culture by culture.

It is not currently considered "politically correct" to reaffirm our colonial Anglo-American cultural roots from New England or Virginia, or Dutch-American roots from New York, or German-American roots from Pennsylvania, or even Scandinavian-American roots. Significantly those are the United States cultures most strongly influenced by the Christianity emerging from the Protestant Reformation, imperfect as that Christian movement might be.

Rather, the new cultural excitement in the United States seems to be revolving around minority cultures such as American Indians in numerous tribal forms, African-Americans, and various Asian-Americans. Among Hispanic-Americans a trend has developed to disparage the European Spanish heritage and emphasize the native Aztec, Mayan or Inca roots. As our understanding of the visible and the invisible reveals, such cultural reaffirmation can be seen as creative steps forward for our nation but it also can be an invitation to serious spiritual downfall.

The step forward, as has been stressed, is bringing to light the redemptive gifts God has implanted in every culture to glorify Himself. Our cultures are intrinsically good because they reflect the Creator. We should affirm this in every United States culture.

But we need also to recognize that Satan has so corrupted cultures that some of their forms such as art and architecture, and particularly some of their behavior patterns such as dances and religious rituals, are clearly intended to glorify the creature rather than the Creator. Cultures whose religious roots exalt demon spirits need to be reaffirmed as cautiously in the United States as they should have been in Haiti and Japan. Otherwise, the invisible forces of darkness thus invited into national life will certainly proliferate and provoke the wrath of God. He will not stand for spiritual harlotry in the United States any more than He did in Judah in Jeremiah's time, and divine judgment is the predictable outcome. Sadly, rather than relieving human suffering, we may well see it increase.

Is Hawaii in Danger?

Hawaii, our fiftieth state, now has a strong movement among some of its leaders for reaffirmation of Hawaiian culture. On August 21, 1992, the governor of Hawaii, one of their U.S. Senators, and many other officials overtly participated in a ritual of traditional Hawaiian paganism billed as a "healing ceremony" for the uninhabited Kahoolawe Island. The ceremony featured offering coral heads at the altar dedicated to the spirits of darkness and drinking the sacred *'awa*. Parley Kanakaole, the event's leader, interpreted the government officials' actions as meaning, "Yes, I will support the Hawaiian cultural heritage and everything it means to be a *kanaka maoli* (a true Hawaiian)."[7]

A stated purpose of this process was to repair the damage done to Hawaii by Christianity. Reporting on the event, Laurel Murphy says that after the missionaries arrived, "The power of the Hawaiian gods began to die, and along with it, the power of the Hawaiian male." Parley Kanakaole "knew that the new *heiau* [temple] had to be a *mua ha'i kupuna*, the family place of worship in old Hawaii where men called on ancestors for help."[8]

Ironically, the motto of the state of Hawaii is: "The life of the land is perpetuated in righteousness." This reflects God's redemptive gift for Hawaii. It will be perpetuated if Jesus Christ is exalted as the rightful Lord of Hawaii, bringing glory to the Creator. But the opposite is also a possibility: the *death* of the land will be perpetuated in unrighteousness. As was mentioned earlier, the wrath of God is poured out on people, "Who suppress the truth in unrighteousness" (Rom. 1:18) by glorifying the creature rather than the Creator. My prayer is that such will not be the case in Hawaii.

CONCLUSION

Where do we draw the line? Spiritual mapping is an attempt to offer guidelines. It helps us know when we begin to glorify the creature rather than the Creator. It reveals the invisible powers, both good and evil, behind visible features of everyday life. It provides us new tools for engaging and overcoming the enemy, thus opening the way for the spread of God's Kingdom and for His glory to be manifested among the nations.

■ REFLECTION QUESTIONS ■

1. Can you think of any instances, apart from those mentioned in the chapter, where people openly have given glory to the creature rather than the Creator?
2. Think about the demonic names given to the natural features of the Grand Canyon. Why would they produce "righteous rage" in some people?
3. Your city has a redemptive gift. What do you think are some possibilities about what the gift is? How about other nearby cities?
4. Discuss some of the specifics of the dangers of affirming paganism while attempting to reaffirm ancient cultures.
5. Review the cleansing of Wagners' living room. Would you have removed the puma? The masks? The lamps? Why?

Notes
1. Dave and Jane Rumph, "Geographical Idolatry: Does Satan Really Own All This?" *Body Life,* June 1992, p. 13.
2. John Dawson, *Taking Our Cities for God* (Lake Mary, FL: Creation House, 1989), p. 39.
3. Tim Stafford, "Campus Christians and the New Thought Police," *Christianity Today,* February 10, 1992, p. 15.
4. George Barna, *What Americans Believe* (Ventura, CA: Regal Books, 1991), p. 84.
5. Jim Shahim, "Island of Hope," *American Way,* October 1, 1991, p. 57.
6. Howard W. French, "Haiti pays dearly for Aristide's overthrow," *Pasadena Star News,* December 25, 1991, n.p.
7. Laurel Murphy, "Hawaiian leaders, dignitaries, head of Kahoolawe," *Maui News,* August 21, 1992, n.p.
8. Ibid.

Dealing with Strongholds

by Cindy Jacobs

CINDY JACOBS IS A GIFTED PRAYER LEADER AND COFOUNDER
with her husband, Mike, of Generals of Intercession,
an organization networking prayer leaders all over
the globe for strategic intercession for cities, nations and
unreached people groups. Author of Possessing the
Gates of the Enemy (Chosen Books), Cindy travels and
speaks nationally and internationally and has been
instrumental in bringing unity to God's people. She also
serves on the International Board of Women's Aglow Fellowship, and is a convener of the Spiritual Warfare Network of the A.D. 2000 United Prayer Track.

Rosario, Argentina—a city of wealth and beauty to the natural eye. In the summer of 1992, the pastors of Rosario invited me to teach a citywide meeting on "Breaking Occultic Strongholds and Witchcraft." Before going to Argentina, I had been distressed to watch TV news reports of terrible flooding in the Santa Fe province where Rosario is located. As I watched the destruction from the rising waters, I began to wonder if the flooding could be the result of a curse. Could the city be under spiritual attack because of the sins of the people? I pondered these thoughts as we entered the city for the seminar and prayed for the Lord to reveal the secret and hidden things in the city.

On the second day of the seminar, several of us from the Harvest Evangelism team went to lunch with a local pastor. The pastor, a regional representative for Omar Cabrera's church, Vision of the Future (a leading Argentinean church in the area of spiritual warfare), had attended a spiritual warfare seminar I had taught the year before in Mar del Plata. He began to tell me how the city of Rosario had been founded.

It seems that a group of priests were transporting a statue of the Queen of Heaven from one city to another. As they traveled, the statue, an image of the Virgin of Rosario, fell from the cart to the ground four separate times within a short distance. The priests, confident the statue was trying to tell them she wanted this to be her home, established what is now the city of Rosario. So the city's spiritual founder is none other than the Queen of Heaven herself! This was *very* enlightening news. I realized my original suspicion that the city was under a curse could well be correct.

That afternoon I met with Rosario's pastors and a small group of leaders who asked me about praying for their city. I explained to them that mapping the city would help them locate the strongholds. I shared how prayer over gates of hell in a city will release Satan's captives into the Kingdom of God. They were very excited! The excitement increased when the information on the founding of the city was described. Although some leaders had known the Virgin of Rosario was linked with their city, they did not know she had chosen the city as her own. Illumination came to their minds as they realized those statues of this virgin were located in every government office in the city and in the main plaza. Some had even called the Virgin of Rosario the "General of the City."

PRAYING FOR A STRATEGY

After this meeting I went back to my hotel room to pray. I felt that repentance for the idolatry of this virgin had to be a key. I felt such repentance could stop the flooding in the city and perhaps in the whole province. However, I also knew that a dangerous situation might erupt if I publicly exposed the worship of Queen of Heaven as idolatry. Argentina is a Catholic nation where Protestants are considered a sect. Furthermore, the veneration of virgins, such as in Rosario, cuts deep into the heart of the culture. As I studied and prayed, I felt the Lord giving me a strategy.

Later that evening as I walked into the packed theater with my translator, Doris Cabrera, many prayers from my heart were shooting heavenward: "Lord, give me the right words; speak through me. Help Doris translate exactly what I'm saying."

The worship of God in that meeting was tremendous. I delivered my prepared message on spiritual mapping. As I closed the service, I read the Scriptures from Jeremiah 7:16-19, how the worship of the Queen of Heaven provoked God to anger. I carefully explained that the Queen of Heaven is not Mary, the mother of Jesus. In fact, Mary would not want to be called by the name of this demon goddess. I told them we do not honor Mary when we worship her as the Queen of Heaven. Nowhere in the Bible was Mary called the Queen of Heaven. Then I described the judgment against the Philistines for their idolatry in Jeremiah 47:2: "Behold, waters rise up out of the north, and shall be an overflowing flood, and shall overflow the land, and all that is therein; the city, and them that dwell therein" *(KJV)*.

You could have heard a pin drop in that theater! I then asked the pastors to come forward. We had a good representation of Baptists, Nazarenes and other groups, as well as charismatics and Pentecostals. I asked Pastor Norberto Carlini if he would lead a prayer of repentance for the worship and idolatry of the Queen of Heaven and then take the city back for the Lord Jesus. He and the other leaders agreed.

As they knelt to pray, an awesome presence of God came over us. The people humbled themselves and began to weep for the sins of their city. The pastors led a prayer of repentance that thundered with the power and authority of God. Each of the leaders in turn repented and then as a group they took back the city from the Queen of Heaven and placed the government of the city upon the shoulders of King Jesus. The rejoicing resounded to the heavenlies as we worshiped and thanked the Lord for the victory.

The Floods Recede

What happened to the city as a result? Well, one thing was discernible almost immediately. As I flew home a few days later I happened to read the *Buenos Aires Herald*. One of the articles said:

> **Delta Floods Stable!** In Santa Fe, Civil Defense officials announced the Paraná River crest had finally begun moving south, bringing instant relief to the population of the province which has daily faced the threat of new evacuation. The river levels had been rising steadily in that district for the past two weeks.[1]

The Paraná water level fell considerably in the provincial capital of Santa Fe, and in Rosario. This was evidence in the visible realm that the curse had been broken and the city released! What a testimony to the power of repentance! God's blessing was released on the city as the stronghold of idolatry was broken.

WHAT IS SPIRITUAL MAPPING?

How did we discover the stronghold of the worship of the Queen of Heaven in Rosario? By something we now call "spiritual mapping." To my knowledge, the first person to use the term "spiritual mapping" was George Otis, Jr. in his book *The Last of the Giants* (Chosen Books). Although many of us who minister in the field of spiritual warfare have been teaching about researching cities to discover strongholds for some time; "spiritual mapping" has now become the acceptable term for such spiritual research.

To be honest, I had some reservations about the term when I first heard it. It sounded a bit New Age to me. I expressed my opinion to several other Christian leaders and I spent some time praying about it. Finally I came to the conclusion that "spiritual mapping" really is a good descriptive title for researching a city.

What exactly is spiritual mapping? In my opinion, it is the researching of a city to discover any inroads Satan has made, which prevent the spread of the gospel and the evangelization of a city for Christ. George Otis, Jr. says it allows us to see our city as it really is—not as it appears to be.[2]

How do you see your city? Many pastors have been called to churches in cities or towns that appear to be quiet and peaceful, only to discover this is far from the truth. Others spend years in violent urban centers with little harvest and finally give up and leave burned out and discouraged. Some have tried to do spiritual warfare but felt they were mostly shadowboxing against unseen forces that attacked their church and families with a vengeance. It does not have to be this way. God is a master strategist. There are principles in the Word of God to help us wage war against the strongholds of Satan, tear down his fortresses and release the captives.

A question often asked when discussing this subject is: "Doesn't the Bible say the earth is the Lord's, and everything in it, and all who live in it?" This, of course, is true. God owns the earth. It is also true, however, that Satan has come along and made false claims. In 2 Corinthians 4:4, the Bible says that Satan has declared himself the god of this world. He has effectively taken captive whole kingdoms. Realistically, most Christians would look at their city and say, "I know the earth is the Lord's, but what has happened to my city?" Unfortunately, most do not know how to change the situation.

I sense a fresh awakening concerning our responsibility to pray for our cities and nations. A couple of years ago as the conveners of the Spiritual Warfare Network were meeting, the Lord impressed on me that a reformation was occurring throughout the churches. The battle cry for this new reformation is, "We wrestle not against flesh and blood, but against principalities, against powers" (Eph. 6:12, *KJV*) and, "The weapons of our warfare are not carnal" (2 Cor. 10:4, *KJV*). We have tried many techniques in evangelism. Why not also try prayer?

Why do some Christians struggle with the concept of dealing with the invisible realm? Charles Kraft of Fuller Theological Seminary has many insightful points on this question in his book *Christianity with Power*. According to Kraft we see what we are taught to see. We interpret reality in culturally approved ways, and we are taught to see selectively. This selective seeing for many European and American societies is conditioned by our "Western worldview." This worldview causes us to believe that only what we are taught through science or what we can discern with our five senses is real. Kraft goes on to state: "We are taught to believe only in visible things. 'Seeing is believing,' we are told. If we can see it, then it must exist. If we can't see it, it must not exist."[3]

NEW TESTAMENT BACKGROUNDS

How much does this Western worldview affect us in the church? In some cases, quite a bit. Some even relegate the territorial powers listed in Ephesians 6:12 to the realm of mythology. Yet Paul tells us we *wrestle* against these "principalities and powers." If there are indeed principalities and powers against which we wrestle, should we not do so with knowledge?

It is interesting to note the number of scholarly books now being published that help open our eyes to the world as Paul must have seen it. Some of the best are being written by Clinton Arnold, who teaches New Testament at Talbot School of Theology. Arnold examines first century Greek, Roman and Jewish beliefs as well as Jesus' teaching about magic, sorcery and divination. Paul's writings are full of references that are directly written against the strongholds of his day. For instance, concerning the question of eating meat sacrificed to idols in the church at Corinth in 1 Corinthians 10, Arnold writes: "One of the main principles that guided Paul's reaction to the Corinthian situation was the conviction that demons animate idolatry."[4]

Another fascinating study of demonic strongholds, related to the goddess Diana of Ephesus, can be found in the book, *I Suffer Not a Woman*, coauthored by Richard Clark Kroeger and Catherine Clark Kroeger. Although the thesis of this book deals with the ministry of women in the church, it also provides profound insight into the world of Ephesus, which Paul encountered in Acts 19. It reveals a culture full of magic, sorcery and divination. The Kroegers' scholarly book gives a vivid description of the goddess Diana:

She wore a high crown, modeled to represent the walls of the city of Ephesus; and her breastplate was covered with breast-like protuberances. Above these she wore a necklace of acorns, sometimes surrounded by the signs of the zodiac; for Artemis (Diana) controlled the heavenly bodies of the universe. On the front of her stiff narrow skirt were rows of triplet animals, and on the sides bees and rosettes—an indication of her dominion over childbirth, animal life, and fertility. An elaborate system of magic developed upon the *Ephesia Grammata,* the six mystic words written on the cult statue of the goddess. The book of Acts tells us that newly converted Christians repudiated this system and burned their costly books of magic (Acts 19:19).[5]

It was not necessary for Paul and his colleagues to visit the library and research the history of Ephesus to discover what invisible powers operated behind the visible aspects of the city. The citizens of Ephesus knew that the territorial spirit ruling their city was Diana as well as citizens of Dallas today know their football team is the Cowboys. Our need for spiritual mapping is more crucial to us mainly because of our Western worldview, which tends to question whether the invisible powers even exist. Paul had no such problem. Nor, by the way, did Luke, as Yale scholar Susan Garrett demonstrates in her excellent book, *The Demise of the Devil.*[6]

STRONGHOLDS

"Stronghold" seems to be a somewhat ambiguous term in much usage today. We need to be clear on the meaning. A stronghold is a fortified place that Satan builds to exalt himself against the knowledge and plans of God.

An important thing to keep in mind is that Satan tries to

conceal the fact that these strongholds exist. He cleverly cloaks them under the guise of "culture." As Peter Wagner points out in the preceding chapter, there is a resurgence of worship of the ancient gods in cultures all across the world. This is a strategy of the enemy to re-empower the demonic principalities over the nations. It is essential, particularly in this age, to learn to evaluate our culture in the light of God's Word. Only under the scrutiny of the lamp of God's revelation will we be able to free the cities and nations of the world from the powers of darkness in order to ready them for spiritual harvest. I am not trying to say that we are going to drive every single demonic force from the earth forever. Even Jesus could not do that. However, our prayers will release regions from the influence of these powers for a season while we go in and harvest.

It is now common for missionaries trained in anthropology to study the culture of the people to whom they are sent for ministry. These principles have been clearly stated by experts in the field in dealing with unreached people groups. One of the best is John Robb's, *The Power of People Group Thinking.*[7] In years past, many mistakes were made by well-meaning missionaries who did not understand the culture of the people group among whom they labored. We do not wish to blame these early missionaries, but neither do we want to repeat their mistakes.

Today, missionaries may know how to analyze cultures, but many do not understand the need to identify the powers behind the formation of the culture. Perhaps one stronghold we should explore is the idolatry of culture itself. Not everything in the culture of a people is necessarily godly! We are sending missionaries into nations where the demonic strongholds are deeply entrenched but we provide them with little or no strategic intercession for the nation or for their families. Many of them have no tools to recognize a demonic stronghold much less to deal with it strategically.

Specific strongholds need to be torn down to release the harvest in our cities and nations. First, it is important to realize that strongholds exist on both personal and corporate levels. We are much more familiar with the personal level than with the corporate levels. The corporate level is the one dealt with by both Daniel and Nehemiah in praying for their nation.

Spiritual warfare is not a big "power trip." Rather, it is displaying God's attributes and ways before a dying, lost world, looking to see if we really are overcomers, not subject to the wicked powers of this age.

In this chapter, I will specifically examine nine strongholds. George Otis, Jr. deals with a tenth, territorial strongholds, in chapter 1. Although this certainly is not an all-inclusive list, these are the strongholds I have most clearly identified up to this point.

1. Personal Strongholds

In his excellent book *Overcoming the Dominion of Darkness*, Gary Kinnaman describes personal strongholds as things that Satan builds to influence one's personal life: personal sin, thoughts, feelings, attitudes and behavior patterns.[8]

One of the Lord's ways of dealing with personal strongholds is through applying biblical standards of holiness. I believe this is an important gateway to revival. In studying the great revivals, one almost invariably reads about sweeping moves of holiness. I explain this in detail in my book *Possessing the Gates of the Enemy* (Chosen Books), in the chapter "The Clean Heart Principle."

One of the greatest hindrances to God's moving in our cities is the pride of the believers. It is time to cry out to God to take the blinders off our eyes so we can see our selfishness, bad attitudes, and lack of character and integrity. I like what I heard Bill Gothard say: "Maturity is doing the right thing, even when no one else is looking!" Our actions are seen by a holy God and the host of heaven.

We need to imitate the character and righteousness of God. Spiritual warfare is not a big "power trip." Rather, it is displaying God's attributes and ways before a dying, lost world looking to see if we really are overcomers, not subject to the wicked powers of this age.

These personal strongholds are "holes in our armor." I first learned this principle from Joy Dawson, a great Bible teacher. Joy says that when we have wrong heart motives such as pride or selfish actions, these are holes in our armor and leave us open to enemy attack. They are closed by repentance before a holy God and by repentance to others we have offended. God only exalts and gives victory to the humble. Through humility, repentance and holiness, personal strongholds can be torn down.

2. Strongholds of the Mind

My friend Ed Silvoso says, "A stronghold is a mind set impregnated with hopelessness that causes the believer to accept as unchangeable something that he or she knows is contrary to the will of God."[9] This is the best definition I have found.

Strongholds can be built in our minds in many ways. The enemy may have us convinced that our city can never be won for the gospel. He likes to set limits on the things we will believe in. Is it possible for a city to be won for Christ? Can the mayor, city council, police force, lawyers and teachers be influenced by the gospel? Of course! Sometimes we are simply "prisoners of war" in our churches. Satan does not mind if we have a little bread and water and a few visitors but gets very unhappy if we determine to influence our whole city. We need to stage a grand prison break! First we must tear down the fortresses built in our minds that it cannot be done.

At one time in my life I had a situation that seemed irreparable. A friend had done something that hurt me deeply, and I felt betrayed. The circumstances were such that it appeared nothing could remedy the problem. For two years I did not see this friend, and we did not talk. Restoration of the relationship looked hopeless on this side of heaven. I did not realize at the time that I had a stronghold that had worked its way into my mind. Satan had tricked me into believing it was an unchangeable situation. This stronghold exalted itself against the knowledge of God that says, "All things are possible to them that believe." Obviously, because of my hurt, I chose not to believe God's promise. I was crippled in this area of my life.

One day as I was praying it came to me that I had believed a lie. Nothing was impossible for God! I began to seek the Lord for a strategy to mend the breach. I felt I needed to discuss the situation with the person and make things right between us. It was not easy. I had to come to a place of forgiveness and healing. Finally, I knew what I should do. I wrote a letter briefly stating my love, and my grief at the situation. In addition, I explained in a nonaccusatory way the situation as I saw it. I ended the letter by asking the person if we could talk by phone as we lived quite a distance from each other. After receiving the letter the person called, and the love of God was so strong during our conversation that the situation was completely remedied and our relationship was restored.

3. Ideological Strongholds

Gary Kinnaman says ideological strongholds "concern world view. Men such as Karl Marx, Charles Darwin, and others particularly affected the philosophies and religious or non-religious views which influence culture and society."[10]

Ideological strongholds are potentially able to affect whole cultures. Adolf Hitler is a prime example of this. Books about Hitler and the Third Reich are revealing and bring to light the occultic power behind the Third Reich that essentially bewitched an entire nation.

Philosophies such as humanism are powerful and seductive. New Age is on the rise and is probably one of the most serious threats to Christianity in the nations of the earth. Those in New Age are taught that they can call upon the power of the demonic forces in *any religion* of the world. They are swiftly infiltrating the schools in many nations in order to take over the minds of our children and set up their ideologies in local and national governments.

We need to understand that these ideological strongholds are inspired by the invisible forces and powers of darkness, which cause the creation of social structures and institutions to carry out their purposes. It cannot be said enough: *We do not wrestle against flesh and blood.* These strongholds must be attacked in nonstop, focused, intelligent, sustained intercession by the churches of the nations.

The fortress-mentality church says we are not responsible for anything outside our four walls and blinds our eyes from seeing the real battle for our cities. Many pastors and leaders are now waking up to realize they have been fighting *off* Satan rather than fighting *against* him!

4. Occultic Strongholds

I see occultic strongholds as an overt evil application of many ideological strongholds. Occultic strongholds are strongholds of witchcraft, satanism and New Age religions, which invite spirit guides to operate. They work as "power boosters" to the territorial spirits that dwell over geographic regions.

The territorial spirits over a city or region are greatly empowered by the occult spells, curses, rituals and fetishes used by witches, warlocks and satanists. Ruling powers of darkness manipulate those involved in the occult to do their bidding and attempt to destroy the power of the church and the reign of God in an area. Christian leaders are often unaware that this is really happening in their city. Many pastors and leaders are themselves under tremendous satanic attack and either they do not realize what is going on or they are so beat-up, discouraged and weary that they cannot fight the onslaught. This is not something we need to fear, but we do need to understand and fight against the wiles or methods of the enemy.

One of the ways those in the occult assault Christians and leaders is by sending curses. This is done through spells, unholy intercession and fastings. Ezekiel 13:18 says: "Woe to the women who sew magic charms on their sleeves and make veils for the heads of people of every height to hunt souls!" Dick Bernal, our colleague in the Spiritual Warfare Network, has written a fine book on the subject: *Curses: What They Are and How to Break Them.*[11]

Evidently sending curses was practiced in both Old and New Testament times (e.g., Isa. 8:19-22; Acts 19:19). It also happens today as we see many Christian leaders fall into sexual sin and immorality. Leaders need intercessors who guard them in prayer against these curses. Peter Wagner's book *Prayer Shield* (Regal Books) deals with this subject in depth.

How can it be determined if someone has been cursed? Here are a few possible symptoms:

- Sickness and infirmity without a natural cause;
- Confusion of the mind (may be caused by mind control);
- Sleeplessness;
- Sexually explicit dreams on a recurring basis;

- Extreme weariness;
- Unexplainable negative attitudes.

I am aware that the things I have suggested can have other causes as well. One way to know whether or not a problem is the result of a curse is that when its power is broken the symptoms disappear quickly. An exception to this can be an occasion when the infirmity from the curse has caused actual physical damage to the body and the body needs healing in addition to having the curse broken.

A curse from Argentina. One of the assignments we deal with in Generals of Intercession is discerning and tearing down the strongholds over cities. In 1990, my friend Doris Wagner and I went to the city of Resistencia, Argentina, to pray with the leaders, teach and discern the strongholds over the city. Victor Lorenzo refers to this visit in his chapter (see chapter 7). One particularly nasty territorial spirit was *San la Muerte,* literally, Saint Death. Thirteen temples were located throughout the city specifically for the worship of *San la Muerte.* Life was so hopeless there the people believed that if they worshiped *San la Muerte* they would at least have a good death:

When I arrived home from the prayer trip, I came under heavy attack. One Sunday I got up for church, went to the service feeling fine, and in the middle of the service started losing the strength in my body. At first I simply thought I was overly fatigued, but as the day progressed I could tell something was seriously wrong with me. Finally I told my husband, Mike, "Honey, call our intercessors and start the emergency prayer chain. I feel like I'm dying!" This was unusual. I had never felt like that in my life, and my husband had never heard me say anything like that before. Because he loves me dearly, he quickly called the intercessors of Generals of Intercession to action. By the time another hour had gone by I could tell the curse had been broken. The next day I felt totally well and strong.

After I recovered, something really bothered me. What right did that curse have to hit me? The Bible says in Proverbs 26:2, "A curse without cause shall not alight." I knew there must be a hole in my armor somewhere. As I continued to pray, the Lord reminded me of a phone call I received the day before from someone very close to my heart. This person told me I was totally wrong to teach on spiritual warfare and I needed to quit.

God showed me then that I had unforgiveness against that person. I had not thought to forgive at the time, but now I suddenly realized this was true! I had sin in my heart. I quickly forgave and went to two friends to ask them to pray with me for the Lord to heal my broken heart. The very next day the person who had hurt me called and asked my forgiveness. The person had simply been used as a tool of the enemy and had deeply repented, as I had done.

5. Social Strongholds

A social stronghold is the oppression over a city in which social injustice, racism and poverty—with their related problems— cause people to believe God does not care about their needs.

The church is slowly waking up to its responsibility to address this stronghold. Scholars such as Walter Wink and Ron Sider are leading the way. Romans 12:21 gives biblical principles for our proper response: "Be not overcome of evil, but overcome evil with good" *(KJV)*.

Ways to demolish this stronghold are through giving to the poor, sheltering the homeless, reconciling the races and clothing those in need. Jesus wants us to identify with the poor and oppressed and engage in whatever social and political action we can, using spiritual weapons of repentance and intercession. This demonstration of God's love is powerful to weaken the enemy.

6. Strongholds Between City and Church

Satan has driven wedges between the Church and the city, which create an "us against them" mentality. The Church often sees city government as its enemy and the city often views the Church in a negative light. This stronghold is torn down when the Church learns to be a blessing to the city.

The Church should be one of the first institutions that city leaders turn to in time of trouble. Instead, it is often the last or it is not contacted at all. To build good rapport with the city, some churches hold banquets for the local police, or give special gifts to the city, or sponsor projects that bless the city such as donating parks for the underprivileged.

The business community often views Christians as the cheapest, stingiest people around. Many waitresses do not like Christians because they are big complainers and small tippers. We must remember we are the only Bible some will ever read.

Some churches shame cities through the sins of their leaders or become an embarrassment to the community. Perhaps some pastors need to go to their city leaders and repent for the iniquities of their church in a way the leaders will relate to. Being willing to build a good relationship between church and city tears down Satan's strongholds in the minds of city leaders, and stops his ability to accuse us before our cities.

7. Seats of Satan

A seat of Satan is a geographic location that is highly oppressed and demonically controlled by a certain dark principality. From this demonic seat, the enemy conducts warfare on the city or nation.

In Revelation 2:13, the Bible speaks of this type of stronghold, which existed in the city of Pergamos. It seems the Lord was trying to reveal to us the strategy employed by the enemy to build fortresses for the worship of demonic gods in certain regions.

The city of La Plata, Argentina, is a seat of Satan for Freemasonry. The whole city was built as a temple for the worship of the spirits connected with Freemasonry. The streets are laid out

---

The Church is God's power plant in the nations to destroy the works of the evil one. It is now waking up to the most powerful weapon in its arsenal—unity.

---

according to Masonic symbols in patterns of diagonals and plazas on every sixth street. Victor Lorenzo's chapter details the spiritual mapping of this seat of Satan (see chapter 7).

8. Sectarian Strongholds

Sectarian strongholds cause divisions among churches, pride in doctrine and beliefs, and idolatry of denominations or particular belief systems that produce isolation from the rest of the Body of Christ.

The dictionary definition of a sectarian is: "One characterized by a narrow or factional viewpoint; of a schismatic religious body; narrow-minded."

I believe sectarian strongholds are often the most critical strongholds. The Bible says a house divided against itself shall fall (see Mark 3:25). Many churches *are* divided. Satan has sent his top guerrilla experts to blow up unity among covenantal friends and, in some cases, has succeeded in a few skirmishes in our cities; but he has not yet won the war—nor will he!

The Church is God's power plant in the nations to destroy

the works of the evil one. It is now waking up to the most powerful weapon in its arsenal—unity.

This is not a new message to the Church. It has been preached for years. I have a theory regarding our inability to achieve unity cross-denominationally sooner: We were so busy fighting within our own denominations, we could not handle adding any more variables to the situation.

Unity is critical as we seek to take the promised lands of our cities. Let's examine the pattern for taking the Promised Land given us in the book of Joshua:

A. All the tribes went in together. Who are the tribes today? The tribe of Baptist, the tribe of Nazarene, the Pentecostal, Congregationalist, charismatics and on and on.

B. They all went at the same time. This was necessary because each tribe had special abilities necessary to take the land.

I used to be naive enough to think the devil invented the various denominations. Only *my* mainline evangelical denomination was going to bring revival. When everyone became just like us, then God could work. I did not know I had a sectarian stronghold. Then I got swept into charismatic renewal and I thought *we* were the ones who were going to bring revival and everyone else was missing it. I traded labels but kept the same stronghold. Finally, the Lord began to convict me of my sectarianism.

C. The priests went first with the Ark. Notice the water did not part until a leader from each tribe also went with the Ark into the Jordan (see Josh. 3:9-17). Many times the people in the congregation are more willing to get together in unity than the leaders, but it is essential that the leaders lead. Several possible reasons for the leaders' unwillingness to unite are:

- Pride of doctrine;
- Fear of rejection;

- Idolatry of denomination or movement;
- Fear of losing members;
- Exhaustion from other ministry demands.

One way the Lord dealt with my sectarian stronghold was to cause me to think about eternal doctrine. You may not have thought about eternal doctrine prior to this and so allow me to ask you a question: When you stand before the throne of God, what is He going to ask you about what you believed? Will He ask you how you were baptized, or how you took communion? Will He ask you what you believe about the gifts of the Spirit? Is He going to want to know if you spoke in tongues?

I do not think so. As He looks for your name in the Lamb's Book of Life, He will more likely ask, "Are you born again? Have you been washed in the blood of the Lamb?" This is *eternal doctrine*. Sectarian strongholds keep us blind to such things.

9. Strongholds of Iniquities

Strongholds of iniquity come from the sins of the fathers that produce iniquities or weaknesses toward certain types of sin in the succeeding generations.

My first understanding of this came through dealing with personal generational iniquities. Later I came to understand these iniquities also work in cultures and bring bondage, sometimes even cursing whole nations through the sins of their fathers. They also affect denominations and churches where the sins of the leaders have become strongholds or iniquities in the succeeding generations of the church. This can open a door for demonic powers to bring sin into the church. These iniquities are often concealed through traditions of the church.

The stronghold of tradition can produce legalism. Cultures that have roots in veneration of ancestors are particularly susceptible to this. One church in another nation refused to dig up a huge, decayed tree stump to make way for a new building because the founder of the church had planted the tree 90 years before. This type of legalism left them susceptible to demonic bondage.

Another church had a history of sexual sin. The pastors and leaders repented for these sins in the life of their church. They went so far as to remove the cornerstone from their building laid by a pastor who was in serious deception. They put a new one in with the name of Jesus on it. They then commanded that all defilement and sin of the spiritual father of their church be broken. As a result, they broke the power of sexual sin in their church. The spiritual atmosphere changed.

Nations also have iniquities. The sins of the fathers of a nation and the people in the nation can bring it under judgment. Many today are praying the Scripture from 2 Chronicles 7:14: "If My people who are called by My name will humble themselves, and pray and seek My face, and turn from their wicked ways, then I will hear from heaven, and will forgive their sin and heal their land."

"Heal their land." This is an interesting concept. Daniel understood this well when he was praying and cried out to God, "We have sinned and committed iniquity" (Dan. 9:5).

Nehemiah confessed to the Lord, "Both my father's house and I have sinned" (Neh. 1:6). He also confessed the sins of Israel, his nation.

The sins of nations can produce national strongholds. These affect many aspects of the culture of the people who live in the nation. These sins can also give the territorial powers legal right to demonize their cultures.

These are the gates of hell. We could stand on the street corner all day and yell at the devil to leave our city, but we are just acting out of presumption and making noise if he has a legal right to rule through the sins of the people within the city.

What are the sins of nations that produce strongholds? How

can we discover a nation's iniquities? What steps do we take in prayer to turn from our wicked ways and break the iniquities of our nations? These are chief questions in spiritual mapping. Some of the answers will be described in detail in the second section of this book.

▰ REFLECTION QUESTIONS ▰

1. Cindy Jacobs believes that the flooding stopped in Rosario, Argentina, because through prayer a curse on the city had been broken. Do you agree. Why?
2. We are taught that "seeing is believing." Talk about some of the fallacies in this statement in light of this chapter.
3. Cindy Jacobs explains nine different kinds of strongholds. Try to verbalize what a stronghold in general is. How would you explain it to a friend?
4. Read aloud the names of the nine kinds of strongholds. How many can you apply to your own city? Describe those that apply the best you can.
5. Do you have a stronghold of sectarianism in your city? If so, what concrete steps could be taken in the next six months to weaken it?

Notes
1. "Delta Floods Stable," *Buenos Aires Herald,* Sunday, June 28, 1992, p. 4.
2. George Otis, Jr., *The Last of the Giants* (Tarrytown, NY: Chosen Books, 1991), p. 85.
3. Charles Kraft, *Christianity with Power* (Ann Arbor, MI: Servant Publications, 1989), p. 24.
4. Clinton Arnold, *Powers of Darkness* (Downers Grove, IL: InterVarsity Press, 1992), p. 97. See also *Ephesians: Power and Magic* (Grand Rapids, MI: Baker Book House, 1992).
5. Richard Clark Kroeger and Catherine Clark Kroeger, *I Suffer Not a Woman* (Grand Rapids, MI: Baker Book House), pp. 53,54.
6. Susan R. Garrett, *The Demise of the Devil* (Minneapolis, MN: Fortress Press, 1989).

7. John Robb, *Focus! The Power of People Group Thinking* (Monrovia, CA: MARC, 1989).
8. Gary Kinnaman, *Overcoming the Dominion of Darkness* (Tarrytown, NY: Chosen Books, 1990), pp. 54,56-58.
9. Edgardo Silvoso (taken from a memorandum to supporters and friends on "Plan Resistencia") September 15, 1990, p. 3.
10. Kinnaman, pp. 162,163.
11. Dick Bernal, *Curses: What They Are and How to Break Them* (Companion Press, Box 351, Shippensburg, PA 17257-0351).

Spiritual Mapping for Prophetic Prayer Actions

by Kjell Sjöberg

K*JELL Sjöberg has been recognized for years as a pioneer in strategic-level spiritual warfare. After being leader for Intercessors for Sweden for 10 years, he has traveled to many nations of the world to teach advanced seminars on prayer and to lead prayer teams. Author of* Winning the Prayer War *(Sovereign World), Kjell (pronounced "Shell") is also the national coordinator for Sweden of the Spiritual Warfare Network of the A.D. 2000 United Prayer Track.*

"Spiritual mapping" is a term coined to cover the research we do preceding what I like to call a "prayer action." Obviously, when we pray we can pray more effectively if we are better informed.

A PRAYING PEOPLE WELL INFORMED

An intercessor friend of mine who is also a businessman had an opportunity to meet our prime minister and present an industrial project to him. He arrived well prepared with documentation and was ready to answer any technical or economic question the prime minister might ask.

Shortly afterward he was seeking the Lord in an area for prayer. He felt that the Lord spoke to him and asked him some questions. "Do you remember when you visited your prime minister? How did you prepare yourself for that meeting? Today you are seeking My face in a very important matter. I am the King of kings. How much have you prepared yourself to be well informed about the area you are presenting to Me?" My friend honestly confessed: "I have not prepared myself in the same way as when I met the prime minister." He felt that the Lord was saying: "Come back another time and be better prepared because before I answer your prayer, I want you to be fully informed."

Intercessors read newspapers and watch TV news and from them receive specific prayer burdens. Most intercessors are eager to follow the news because answers to prayer are often reported on the front page of the newspaper. I challenge intercessors who take responsibility for cities or nations to become as well informed as a police officer or the editor of a newspaper.

There was a time when Intercessors for Sweden, the ministry I serve, had a "shadow cabinet" of men and women who took responsibility for each portfolio in the government. They were appointed as watchers responsible for providing information to those who were praying for the nation. One was responsible for environment, another for industry and trade, a third for agriculture and so on.

We can pray in the spirit and get information from the Holy Spirit, but we must also pray with our understanding. The basic concept of spiritual mapping is that we need to be as well informed as possible when we are praying.

PEOPLE WITH A GIFT FOR MAPPING

When I choose the team members for a given prayer action, I attempt to bring together people with a variety of spiritual gifts. A pastor is needed among the prayer warriors, one who is responsible for our protection and who can care for the weak, the tired and the wounded. Others are gifted for spiritual mapping. I have had a bold master spy on my team.

Once when a spiritist world congress was held in Sweden, our master spy felt led to register as a delegate. At the same time, he called for a prayer conference in a nearby church. He attended the sessions in the spiritist congress, gathered information, and then walked over to the church to inform the intercessors who used it for spiritual warfare. The spiritist congress ended up a failure and an economic disaster.

I would not recommend that everyone do what he did. He is one of the few who has such gifts and calling of God. Without God's direction these activities can be presumptuous and dangerous.

In order to spy on a society in Sweden that is attempting to revive the ancient religion of the Vikings and is worshiping the Asa-gods, this same spy intercessor became a member of the society. Of course he did not use his real name. On his door he had two interchangeable nameplates. He is always well informed about the activities of New Age groups and satanists and he has a nose to track down the information that prayer warriors need.

Nowadays when we have a prayer conference or plan for a prayer action, we usually have a research paper prepared ahead of time dealing with the history of the city from a spiritual perspective. This gives the prayer warriors a more thorough understanding of the battlefield they are about to enter.

SPIRITUAL MAPPING IN BERGSLAGEN, SWEDEN

We have an area in Sweden called Bergslagen, where church membership was decreasing and many were unemployed. A decision was made to shut down the iron mill that had about 600 iron workers. One Sunday evening the whole town of Grängesberg protested by turning out all electric lights in homes, streets and shops. The TV news showed a town in darkness. It was a demonstration of hopelessness—people saw no future for the town. The price of property fell and it was almost impossible to sell a house.

At that time we decided to initiate six months of warfare prayer and finish our prayer campaign with a weekend of victory proclamations of hope for the future. My friend Lars Widerberg, the spy in our prayer team, did the spiritual mapping and discovered there were 15 New Age centers in the area. Every time through history when our nation's freedom had been threatened, the farmers from Bergslagen became the freedom fighters who saved the country. Bergslagen was the birthplace of industry in Sweden and now it was heading for oblivion.

The first factory in Sweden's history was now occupied by a community connected with the Findhorn Foundation from England, which confesses that Lucifer is their source of power. We went into the Lucifer center and had coffee. To outsiders we appeared as a group in pleasant conversation while we were looking into the eyes of one another and proclaiming the Lordship of Jesus over the community. Two months later four members of that community came to the Lord and were filled with the Holy Spirit. The Lord gave us the spoils from our prayer action.

Lars also discovered that in the Bergslagen area lived a spiritist medium who claimed to be a channel for the spirit of Jambres, an Egyptian who had lived 3,000 years ago. We organized a prayer bus filled with intercessors and stopped outside of every New Age center in the city to pray. The prayer bus also stopped outside every town hall in the area. We prayed that the local political leadership would receive wisdom from God to solve the problems of unemployment in the area. We prayed that they would use public funds with wisdom and honesty. We did spiritual warfare against the spirit of Jambres. Jambres was one of the Egyptian magicians who withstood Moses and Aaron to hinder the Exodus from Egypt.

We had a tough battle and went through a fire of opposition from the local media, who could not understand our boldness to proclaim a new day for Bergslagen. That evening when we directly challenged the spirit of Jambres, opposition started and increased until the weekend when we proclaimed a new day for Bergslagen. The opposition helped us believe that we had hit the target. Jambres may well have been the territorial spirit over the area.

The day after the victory proclamation the government gave a grant of one billion Swedish crowns (150 million U.S. dollars) to the whole area. Immediately prices of property went up and unemployment went down. The iron mill closed, but all the workers got new jobs. Our prayer action drew pastors and churches into unity and they kept on praying together. When the media reported the changes in the area, they used the same words we had used in our prayer proclamations, but of course they reported no cause-and-effect relationships.

PRAYER AND GEOGRAPHY

Prayer has a geographical dimension and therefore many experienced intercessors are interested in maps. The walls of my prayer room are covered with maps. On one wall I have a world map; on the other wall is a huge map of Stockholm. I have been encouraged by some of my friends who also have maps in their prayer rooms. Many times I stand in front of the world map when I am praying.

When I was young, Watchman Nee opened up my eyes for the geographical dimension of prayer through his book *The Prayer Ministry of the Church.*[1]

> In teaching us to pray "Thy Kingdom come," the Lord is saying that there is a Kingdom of God in heaven, but that on this earth there is not, and that therefore we ought to pray to God to extend the boundary of the Kingdom of the heavens to reach to this earth. The Kingdom of God in the Bible is spoken of in geographical terms as well as in historical terms. History is a matter of time, whereas geography is a matter of space.
>
> According to the Scriptures, the geographical factor of the Kingdom of God exceeds its historical factor. "If I cast out demons by the Spirit of God," said the Lord Jesus, "surely the Kingdom of God has come upon you" (Matt. 12:28). Is this a historical problem? No, it is a geographical problem. Wherever the Son of God casts out demons by the Spirit of God, there is the Kingdom of God. So during this period of time, the Kingdom of God is more geographical than historical. If our concept of the Kingdom is always historical, we have then seen but one side of it, not the whole thing.

The Lord is calling intercessors to take responsibility for cities and nations and people groups. Geographical borders show us our areas of responsibility. According to Acts 17:26,27, the Lord has determined the boundaries of where people live, so that we shall seek the Lord within those boundaries. We have sent prayer teams to pray along the borders of Sweden.

We divided the borders of the coastline into 50 segments and asked a church or a prayer group to walk or travel along that portion of the border and pray.

Sometimes we have stood at borders of areas closed to the gospel and prayed for the nations to open up. Twice before the communist regime fell in Albania I led prayer teams that prayed at the borders of Albania. Others did similar prayer actions. Before Denmark had its referendum, when the majority voted no to the Maastrich agreement to a European union, intercessors did prayer walks along the border between Germany and Denmark because they sensed that the agreement would be a setback for the gospel.

SPIRITUAL GEOGRAPHY IN THE BIBLE

The Bible attributes special spiritual importance to certain geographical sites. For example, the Lord designed a unique spiritual geography for the Promised Land quite different from what we find on ordinary maps. Six cities were chosen as cities of refuge. Forty-eight cities were given to the priests and the Levites. When they moved into the Promised Land, the children of Israel were to seek the place on which the Lord had chosen to put His name for a dwelling. David found that place to be Jerusalem. On some geographical areas a special blessing was proclaimed, such as when Moses blessed Joseph and said: "Blessed of the Lord is his land, with the precious things of heaven, with the dew, and the deep lying beneath, with the precious fruits of the sun...with the precious things of the everlasting hills" (Deut. 33:13-15).

Jacob was met at a border crossing by the angels of God. He said: "This is God's camp." So he named that place Mahanaim, which means "two camps" (see Gen. 32:1,2). Another border crossing was named Mizpah, which means "watch." Laban said: "May the Lord watch between you and me when we are absent one from another" (Gen. 31:49). Jacob proclaimed that at this pillar no one should pass with an evil intent against the other (Gen. 31:48-53).

Samuel set up a stone on the borderline of the Philistines after he had defeated them. He, "Called its name Ebenezer, saying, 'Thus far the Lord has helped us.' So the Philistines were subdued, and they did not come anymore into the territory of Israel" (1 Sam. 7:12,13).

SACRED GEOGRAPHY AND OCCULT CITY PLANNING

American anthropologist Johan Reinhard made an extensive study of the Andes Mountains of Peru and Bolivia. Reporting his findings in *National Geographic*, he concludes, "The landscape was not merely a region of challenging topography, but actually a complex religious map. Mountains were spiritual landmarks fraught with magical significance."[2]

Reinhard reports that the sacred mountains are related to one another under *Illimani*, the chief god of the mountains, to whom we would refer as a territorial spirit. The article is illustrated with maps of the sacred mountains and lakes of the Andes. Of Machu Picchu, the cradle of the Inca Empire, Reinhard says, "The location of Machu Picchu allows for a combination of sacred geography and astronomical alignments that is perhaps unequaled in the Andes."[3]

I become spiritually alert when I read about sacred rivers, lakes, wells, forests, parks, cities and mountains. The Scripture says, "The mountains will bring peace to the people, and the little hills, by righteousness" (Ps. 72:3). Satan wants to block the flow of blessing that God has intended to give through His creation, therefore he draws people into worship of geographical sites. We have seen breakthroughs and a changed atmosphere when we have done warfare prayer at places dedicated to the demons.

When we do spiritual mapping, we often discover occult city planning with roots in Babylon and Egypt in newly built cities and suburbs such as Victor Lorenzo describes in chapter 7. In Babylon, the gates were dedicated to the gods of the city and a ziggurat was placed in the center of Babylon. In many capitals and cities in the world we find obelisks erected, sometimes at the zero point, from where all the distances are measured. An obelisk is a phallic symbol of Freemasonry connected with fertility and a shape that was sacred in antiquity to the Egyptian sun-god *Re* or *Ra*. Obelisks and totem poles are erected as landmarks in the districts of the gods to which they are dedicated.

Transcendental Meditation in Sweden is building a model village in Skokloster under the instructions of Maharishi and according to the Hindu Vedic architecture called *Sthapatya-Veda,* the science of the perfect life environment. This science states that the houses shall greet the sun, therefore they shall all have their entrance to the east. As well, all houses and roads shall be built in a checkered pattern to fit into ley lines and power points in a way so as not to disturb the flow of psychic energy. The village is built with the meditation center in the midst and every house has a small meditation tower.

PROPHETIC PRAYER ACTIONS

Prophetic prayer actions are done only at the Lord's command in His perfect timing according to a strategy the Lord has revealed for the team.

Before Gideon had his army of 300 chosen warriors, he used a smaller strike force of 10 in one of history's first recorded guerrilla actions. Gideon obeyed the Lord's command at night and took 10 of his servants to tear down his father's altar to Baal, cutting down the Asherah pole beside it and building a proper kind of altar to the Lord on the same place. (See Judg. 6:25-27.) This was a divinely appointed prayer action.

Elijah is an example for intercessors. The word of the Lord came to Elijah: "Go down to meet Ahab king of Israel,...He is now in Naboth's vineyard." (See 1 Kings 21:17,18, *NIV.*) Elijah met Ahab just when he came to take possession of the vineyard after Naboth had been murdered. In the same way, the Lord is

---

Part of spiritual mapping is to ask the Lord for prophetic words and visions concerning churches, cities and nations....God raises up intercessors to cooperate with Him, just when changes that may open a nation for the gospel are about to take place.

---

giving us divine assignments to be in the right place for God's timing and for confronting evil in high places.

Prophetic prayer actions are specifically connected with prayer teams sent to the frontlines of nations closed to the gospel. These teams travel to the unreached peoples, into Muslim countries, to disaster areas, to the headquarters of the enemy, to the strongholds of Mammon and to such places where even angels do not like to go.

Prophetic prayer actions often are generated from groups that meet on a regular basis to intercede for cities and nations. Ongoing prayer for cities and nations forms a powerful base from which specific prayer actions are born as the Lord speaks to the group. Then a smaller team is frequently chosen and sent forth on prayer journeys or other assignments.

As a prayer leader, I believe God holds me responsible for the protection of the intercessors on my team. I always ask myself: How far can we go? What are the people prepared for? What time line is God laying out for us? Are these intercessors mature enough in the Spirit to understand the things we are about to do? God shows us many things about warfare prayer that we would not be wise to discuss in a larger prayer gathering. After a large gathering we often call together a smaller number of discerning people for intensive follow-up. At times it is harmful to attract the attention of the public or to allow for media coverage.

WHY DO WE CALL PRAYER ACTIONS PROPHETIC?

In describing some prayer actions, we use the term "prophetic" because we pray for God's prophetic word to be fulfilled. Part of spiritual mapping is to ask the Lord for prophetic words and visions concerning churches, cities and nations. The prophets of the Bible spoke prophetic words over nations in the Middle East such as Iran, Iraq, Lebanon, Israel and Ethiopia. When we recently made a prophetic prayer journey to Egypt, we prayed for the fulfillment of Isaiah 19, a prophecy directed to Egypt. We often use the prophetic word as a weapon in prayer.

A prophetic time dimension in prayer also needs to be considered. The Lord is training us to know His will concerning timing. The Lord wants intercessors to be present at the turning points of history when, "He changes the times and the seasons; He removes kings and raises up kings" (Dan. 2:21). Therefore, God raises up intercessors to cooperate with Him, just when changes that may open a nation for the gospel are about to take place. Before we can start to build and plant, structures in the kingdom of darkness need to be uprooted, torn down, destroyed and overthrown, as God said to Jeremiah (see Jer. 1:10).

Many times the Lord has urged us to gather God's people for prayer on certain dates without us knowing exactly why.

Three times we have been led to call national prayer conferences at the time when New Age groups have held their national conferences. We started and ended at the same time without previously knowing about the New Age program, but somehow we sensed that God wanted us to be in prayer before Him. In Madrid, we even booked the same conference center, large enough for two conferences going on simultaneously!

On occasion, the Lord urges us to pray when there is high level activity in the occult world. These are days when the Kingdom of God is advancing and when new doors are opening up for the Church. The church that slumbers while Satan is active will end up depressed and defeated.

Motivations for Prophetic Prayer Action

Intercessors are called to serve the evangelists and prepare the way for souls to be saved. They are called in a priestly ministry to stand before the Lord as representatives of the people, to confess the sins of the people and to ask for mercy.

Individual sin hinders a person from having close fellowship with God. Collective sin hinders God's Spirit from being manifested over a community. The Lord has planned to fill the whole earth with His glory; but unfortunate things have happened in the past that instead veil His glory. Jesus spoke to the religious leaders in Jerusalem about the collective sin of the city—the sin of not having received those sent by the Lord. "Therefore you are witnesses against yourselves that you are sons of those who murdered the prophets. Fill up, then, the measure of your fathers' guilt" (Matt. 23:31,32).

Guilt that has never been dealt with is an open invitation to demonic powers. Before we can bind the strongman, we need to deal with the sins that have given the enemy a legal right to occupy. The devil and his principalities have been defeated by Jesus on the cross and they would not be able to stay on unless they were relying on old invitations that have never been canceled.

Hosea the prophet accused Israel of not having dealt with a sin that was about 250 years old. "O Israel, you have sinned from the days of Gibeah; there they stood" (Hos. 10:9).

Moses instructed the elders in the city how to deal with corporate sin. After a person has been found slain in the field and it is not known who the murderer is, the elders from the nearest city shall make a sacrifice and pray: "Provide atonement, O Lord, for Your people Israel, whom You have redeemed, and do not lay innocent blood to the charge of Your people Israel." It goes on to say, "And atonement shall be provided on their behalf for the blood. So you shall put away the guilt of innocent blood from among you when you do what is right in the sight of the Lord" (Deut. 21:8,9).

It is important to understand the difference here between individual sin and collective sin. When unbelievers repent and confess their personal sins and believe in Jesus, they are saved. No one else can take their place and confess their sins for them. This, however, is not true for collective sin. Intercessors can confess collective sin even though they did not personally participate in the sin, and something that has displeased God can be removed. When that happens, God can pour out His Holy Spirit. It then becomes easier for unbelievers to hear the gospel of Christ, repent of their personal sins and be saved. This is how strategic-level intercession paves the way for effective evangelism.

Ezra gives us an example. As he was agonizing before God and confessing the sins of his forefathers, he cried, "Since the days of our fathers to this day we have been very guilty, and for our iniquities we, our kings, and our priests have been delivered into the hand of the kings of the lands, to the sword, to captivity, to plunder, and to humiliation, as it is this day" (Ezra 9:7).

SEVEN CRUCIAL QUESTIONS FOR SPIRITUAL MAPPING

Up to this point, I have dealt with some of the fundamental principles of spiritual mapping we have gleaned through years of doing prophetic prayer actions. Through experience, we have gained some insight on what sort of research is more valuable than others in giving direction to pastors and intercessors for taking a city or an area for God. Seven crucial questions that we have found the most helpful have emerged for the kind of warfare prayer God uses my colleagues and me for most consistently. Other questions might be more helpful to those who have other assignments.

1. What are the main gods of the nation?

When the Lord delivered Israel out of Egypt He said: "Against all the gods of Egypt I will execute judgment" (Exod.12:12). When we prayed for freedom for the people in the Soviet Union, we first made a list of their gods and asked the Lord to judge all their gods. When I go to a nation, I usually find out which god the president or the king is worshiping and which gods the business leaders worship.

The Greek god *Hermes,* whose Roman name is *Mercury,* is honored in the business community in many nations. We find his statue in some of the major stock exchanges of the world. *Hermes* is a protector of business people, thieves and orators. He himself was the master thief according to Greek mythology. Behind many idols are demons who demand worship.

We felt led to pray on the spot at the stock exchange in Tokyo, and in the name of Jesus remove *Hermes* as the protector of the thieves. This was at the time of the *Daijosi* ceremony, which Peter Wagner describes (see chapter 2). After November 1990, one case of corruption after another was exposed in the stock exchange in Tokyo. It has never been the same since and is still going down as I write this. God hates greed and perhaps we are seeing judgment.

2. What are the altars, the high places and temples connected with worship to fertility gods?

When Abraham came to the Promised Land, he built an altar to God and called on the name of the Lord. (See Gen. 12:8.) To build an altar was to include the land in the covenant between God and His chosen people. The land became covenanted to the Lord. When heathens build altars to their gods, they covenant the land to their idols and to the dark angels behind them.

The way to possess the land is to, "Utterly destroy all the places where the nations which you shall dispossess served their gods, on the high mountains and on the hills and under every green tree. And you shall destroy their altars, break their sacred pillars, and burn their wooden images with fire; you shall cut down the carved images of their gods and destroy their names from that place" (Deut. 12:2,3). This is a key to opening up nations for the gospel. In New Testament times we do it by warfare prayer. Before a prayer action, we map all the high places and altars dedicated to other gods. We also do research to find out if they have been reactivated and used today by occult groups.

3. Have political leaders, such as a king, president or tribal chief dedicated themselves to a living god?

This is not as uncommon as some might think. Has the founder of the nation been exalted to be worshiped as a god after death? We have found national poets, heroes, saints and generals being elevated to gods after their death. Where kings or political leaders have become gods and accept worship from their subjects, they have taken the place that belongs to Jesus. The emperor of Japan is an example, as Peter Wagner points out (see chapter 2).

Among tribes and nations resistant to the gospel, we often find this loyalty being a hindrance to the freedom of the gospel. This is a method often used today by dictators to create a false unity and blind obedience in a nation. God sent an angel to strike down Herod, who had accepted worship as a living god. After that hindrance had been removed, Luke could write: "But the word of God grew and multiplied" (Acts. 12:24).

4. Has there been bloodshed that pollutes the land?

During the reign of David, famine was existent for three successive years. David sought the face of the Lord. The Lord said, "It is because of Saul and his bloodthirsty house, because he killed the Gibeonites" (2 Sam. 21:1). David dealt with the blood guilt that caused the famine in an Old Testament way, and God answered prayer on behalf of the land. The harvest was saved from further destruction.

5. How was the foundation of the city or nation laid?

"Those from among you shall build the old waste places; you shall raise up the foundations of many generations; and you shall be called the Repairer of the Breach, the Restorer of Streets to Dwell In" (Isa. 58:12).

A research group studied the history of Sydney, Australia, and found that a whole aboriginal tribe was wiped out when Sydney was built. Another city was founded by forgery of land documents. The founder of the city had to flee when it was discovered that those who sold the land had been deceived. In a tribal area, a town was founded through a treaty with the tribe. Soon afterward the treaty was broken, but those who violated the treaty with the tribal people subsequently had streets named after themselves. When the tribal people walk these streets today, they are reminded of the wicked people who deceived them.

Aalborg, Denmark, was originally founded as a slave market

where the Vikings could sell their prisoners of war as slaves. A city founded by such bloodshed and crime has a curse upon it. No wonder churches cannot grow on cursed soil or that a dark angel from Satan could establish his throne from the very beginning. The Lord said through Ezekiel: "I will break down the wall you have plastered with untempered mortar, and bring it down to the ground, so that its foundation will be uncovered" (Ezek. 13:14). Through spiritual mapping, the Lord is today laying foundations bare, as Victor Lorenzo shows concerning La Plata, Argentina (see chapter 7).

6. How have God's messengers been received?
"And whoever will not receive you nor hear your words, when you depart from that house or city, shake off the dust from your feet" (Matt. 10:14). Such an act will bring God's judgment on a city.

I was told by a pastor from Mallakka, Malaysia, that his church did not grow, and other churches in the city did not grow either. Something was blocking their evangelistic efforts. Then a prophet from England came to Mallakka who had read the history of how the Catholic missionary Francis Xavier left Mallakka. The people did not listen to Xavier, so he went up on a mountain and literally shook the dust from his feet. The English prophet took a group of pastors from Mallakka up to that same mountain, where they repented because the city had not received a servant of God more than 400 years ago. The curse was broken and the pastor said that from that day his church began to grow. Other churches and cities are under God's judgment because they did not receive God's servants, and this is the reason the soil is barren.

7. How were the old seats of power built?
Spiritual mapping for prophetic prayer actions brings us into new areas.

For example, in some African nations with a high percentage of Christians, the time is ripe to place more Christians in national leadership positions. When we pray for elections and for Christian candidates, we have discovered that we need to dismantle the old seats of power in order to have godly leaders in authority.

The old seats of power frequently have been built through covenants with idols. The office of the president may have been dedicated to the mightiest territorial spirit of the president's tribe and to the dead—his ancestors. In this way a seat of power has been dedicated to one god after another, and all

---

We need the highest precision of aim to hit the enemy at his most vulnerable point. Wisdom in battle is to win the victory without wasting ammunition.

---

have certain claims to the office. Before a coup to overthrow a president, goats and frogs might have been sacrificed for the success of the coup. Advice might have been taken from a witch doctor, who received a new Mercedes when the coup succeeded. We need mapping of national seats of power so we can pray more effectively. We need to ask: "If places of power have spirits, can they be identified?"

HOW DO WE USE SPIRITUAL MAPPING?

Spiritual mapping is often used as a confirmation of things we have already seen in the Spirit. When our warfare strategy has been confirmed from several sources, we can then move on with greater boldness. If the Lord reveals to us the name of the strongman of a city, it needs to be confirmed from the Scripture and from history. If the strongman has been around for hundreds of years, he has certainly left his footprints in the history and the geography of the city. Everything we need to know about our enemy and his troops is also revealed in the Bible.

We use spiritual mapping when we plan our prayer strategy. What kind of prayer weapons shall we use? What is the character of the battlefield? In what order shall we deal with the prayer issues? Confession must come before the warfare. First we cancel the invitations to the strongman before we can command him to leave. Research helps us with timing and places to visit. Spiritual mapping also shows who should be involved. When we deal with the slave trade issue, for example, we invite representatives of the nations that were involved in slave trade to repent on behalf of their nations. On the occasion when we dealt with the Spanish Inquisition issue, I invited a direct descendent of a Jewish family who was expelled from Spain to participate with the team.

We are not in bondage to our research. We do not use all the material prepared by eager researchers. David had five stones when he met Goliath on the battlefield, but he only used one of his sharp stones to conquer the giant. We need the highest precision of aim to hit the enemy at his most vulnerable point. Wisdom in battle is to win the victory without wasting ammunition.

When we have done research and present our spiritual mapping to the elders of the city I usually ask: "Have you dealt with these things previously in prayer?" We do not want to repeat what pastors and churches have already done. We once went to pastors in the city of Berlin and asked: "Have you dealt with the blood guilt on this city considering that World War II started in Berlin and caused the death of millions of people?"

"We have never thought about it and we have never heard anyone confess this blood guilt in the church," was the answer we received.

Sometimes the mapping uncovers previously unknown facts about areas we have already prayed about. That gives us greater freedom to deal with the area on a new level of understanding.

Praying in Moscow at the KGB Headquarters

In October 1987, we organized a prophetic prayer action in Moscow in connection with the 70-year celebrations of the Soviet Communist Constitution. Daniel knew that the time had come for him to intercede for the release of his people after he discovered the prophetic promise of release after 70 years of captivity in Babylon. The Lord demonstrates His might by setting time limits on the evil powers. The Lord gave us faith that the same time limit had been set for the communist oppression against persecuted Christians and Jewish refusniks. We had discerned five prayer targets for that night in Moscow and one of them was the KGB headquarters.

For this prayer action, research material about the KGB was distributed to the 12 on the prayer team. We listened to a two-hour lecture about the organization of the KGB. The KGB had 19,000 officers and 400,000 agents working in the Soviet Union. All around the world they had half a million informers. The founder was Dzerzinsky and his statue was standing at the square in front of the Ljublanka prison. On the map of Moscow, we pinpointed places connected with the KGB where they trained their agents, and the Lumumba university where they recruited their agents from other nations.

One minute past midnight between October 17 and 18, 1987, we started our prayer action near the KGB headquarters. We had received two words of knowledge from an Israeli intercessor and from a sister in Scotland, both saying that they saw us praying in a tunnel. In front of the KGB headquarters is an underground station with a walking tunnel under the square. We discovered that the tunnel passed right under the statue of

Dzerzinsky. The Lord had provided a place where we could pray in freedom without being disturbed by anyone.

We entered the tunnel, and no one else walked through during the entire time we prayed. Here we proclaimed the *Mene, Mene, Tekel Upharsin,* the handwriting on the wall that had announced the downfall of the Babylonian Empire (see Dan. 5:25). We prayed, "In the name of Jesus we bind you, power of Pharaoh, you controlling power of Assur and we lay you under the feet of Jesus. We proclaim that your grave has been prepared. We cut your influence from the root."

On August 22, 1991, the statue of the founder of the KGB was removed. The secret archives of the KGB have been revealed. No more Christians are in prison. The Jewish refusniks are returning to Israel.

DEALING WITH THE ROOTS OF SLAVERY IN AFRICA

In July 1992, prayer leaders in West Africa called intercessors from around the world to come and help in carrying out a historic intercessory assignment in Nigeria and West Africa. The assignment was to deal with the roots of slavery that still affect the mentality of Africans. Black leaders in Africa have treated their own people in the same way as the white slave traders treated the slaves. Slavery still exists in Mauritania and among some tribes in Sudan.

In preparation for the prayer conference in Lagos we researched the slave trade. Mapping was done of the old slave coast, famous for its slave trade. We gathered information about the slave ports and the fortresses where the slaves were kept in dungeons before they passed the gate of no return. During 400 years, 80 million slaves were shipped out from the island of Goree, near Dakar. It became a cruel place of selection, where they decided which ones would be profitable to ship to the United States. The rest were thrown to the sharks or left to die.

During the time of repentance, we were surprised to see so many Africans confess that their ancestors had been part of taking slaves and selling them to the slave traders. A lady from Ghana wept and confessed that her father had told her with pride how her tribe had sold slaves. Today, the families who profited from selling slaves many generations ago have problems that cannot be solved with money. After the prayer conference that dealt with the roots of slavery through repentance and prayer warfare, we sent out teams to pray at the slave centers and ports along the West African coast.

We feel that this one prophetic prayer journey to West Africa has not torn down all the strongholds the enemy is using to keep large populations of both blacks and whites in bondage. However, some of the corporate sin rooted in the slave trade was certainly confessed and remitted. Much more needs to be done, and I believe it will be done in the fairly near future as the Holy Spirit continues to speak to the churches about strategic-level spiritual warfare. Worldwide, God is raising up huge numbers of intercessors to reinforce the spiritual army. One of the greatest helps to those intercessors will be increasing activity in intelligent spiritual mapping, characterized by discernment and sensitivity to God's timing.

■ REFLECTION QUESTIONS ■

1. Kjell Sjöberg tells of a person who enrolled in a spiritist congress in order to do spiritual espionage. Do you think everybody should do such things? If not, who should and who should not?
2. Discuss the spiritual importance of political borderlines. Why is it meaningful to pray along such borders? What happens?
3. Some of the Old Testament descriptions of prophetic prayer actions seem strange. We don't think often about God still

desiring such things, but apparently it is happening. What is your opinion about doing this today? Give reasons.

4. Attempt to apply Kjell Sjöberg's seven questions to your city or nation one by one.

5. Why do we do spiritual mapping? Review Sjöberg's reasons and discuss them.

Notes

1. Watchman Nee, *The Prayer Ministry of the Church* (New York, NY: Christian Fellowship Publishers, Inc.), p. 47.

2. Johan Reinhard, "Sacred Peaks of the Andes," *National Geographic,* March 1992, p. 93.

3. Ibid., p. 109.

Part II:
The Practice

Defeating the Enemy with the Help of Spiritual Mapping

by Harold Caballeros

*H*AROLD CABALLEROS IS FOUNDER AND PASTOR OF EL SHAD-*dai Church in Guatemala City, a church of several thousand. He was an attorney before God called him into the ministry. He travels widely, teaching spiritual warfare to Christian leaders of many nations. Harold serves as area coordinator for the Spiritual Warfare Network and as Latin American representative for the United Prayer Track of the A.D. 2000 and Beyond Movement. His interdenominational ministry, Jesus Is Lord of Guatemala, has enlisted some 20,000 intercessors in Guatemala.*

The 1991 Persian Gulf War was different from any of the previous wars. Its short duration, the vast and diversified level of technology, and the highly sophisticated communications and information gathering that coordinated the allied forces, all contributed to achieving the goal with very few losses. Most would

---

Spiritual mapping gives us an image or spiritual photograph of the situation in the heavenly places above us. What an X ray is to a physician, spiritual mapping is to intercessors.

---

agree that sophisticated technology was the chief factor that permitted this victory without a great loss of human life.

SPIRITUAL MAPPING

The natural is only a reflection of the spiritual, and a connection between them always exists. We who are interested in spiritual warfare are constantly looking for better spiritual technology. Isaiah 45:1-3 helps us realize that God reveals new information to His people, so that we can perform better in the battle and gain the victory. We can expect that if God would go before Cyrus, "His anointed," He will likely do the same for us today. He will prepare the way for us (v. 2), give us the treasures of *darkness* and the hidden riches of *secret* places (v. 3) in order to subdue nations.

The world's population is ever increasing and we are confronted with an awesome challenge—3.6 billion people who have not yet heard the gospel! However, our God is sovereign and is revealing new and better strategies so that we may reach those billions in our generation. I am convinced that spiritual mapping is one of these revelations. It is one of the secrets of God that helps open our spiritual "radar detectors" to show us the world situation as God sees it, *spiritually*, and not as we usually see it, *naturally*.

If I were to define spiritual mapping, I would say: It is God's revelation about the spiritual situation of the world in which we live. It is a vision that goes beyond our natural senses and, by the Holy Spirit, reveals the spiritual hosts of darkness to us.

Spiritual mapping gives us an image or spiritual photograph of the situation in the heavenly places above us. What an X ray is to a physician, spiritual mapping is to intercessors. It is a supernatural vision that shows us the enemy's lines, location, number, weapons, and above all, how the enemy can be defeated.

Spiritual mapping plays the same important role that intelligence and espionage play during war. It reveals the conditions behind enemy lines. It is a spiritual, strategic and sophisticated tool, which is powerful in God to assist in pulling down the strongholds of the enemy.

We should also take note of another part of our supernatural vision, namely, the millions of angels whom God has sent forth to minister to those who inherit salvation (see Heb. 1:14). Angels obey His calling. They are heavenly warriors who, as a disciplined army, receive their orders from heaven itself. They come to our aid and help defeat the enemy (Dan. 10:13; Ps. 91:11; Rev. 12:7).

Spiritual mapping is a relatively new field in our Christian community, and collectively we are learning a great deal. There is a fairly good consensus, however, on several important theological premises, which I will highlight. They will be helpful to those who seek an introduction to the field.

OUR PRINCIPAL TASK

The people of the world can be divided into two large groups:

1. The believers. Those who, "according to his mercy" are saved, "through the washing of regeneration and renewing of the Holy Spirit" (Titus 3:5). The apostle Paul says they are spiritual beings and, thus, can discern all things spiritually (see 1 Cor. 2:14,15). This is the group we call the Body of Christ, the Church.

2. The unbelievers. Those who have not yet made Jesus Christ the Lord and Savior of their lives. Millions of people who live under the slavery of the devil, of sin and of ignorance, *cannot* free themselves of this enormous bondage.

The unbelievers of the world must be seen as the object of our formidable task. Winning the lost is *the* challenge for all of us as believers, and it is the chief reason for books such as this. Why are we still here on earth? Why aren't we automatically taken to heaven to live with God when we become saved? Can we get "more saved" or "more justified" or "more sanctified" by staying here on earth?

The fundamental objective for the Church here on earth is to accomplish God's purposes. "[He] desires all men to be saved and to come to the knowledge of the truth" (1 Tim. 2:4). And, "The Lord is not slack concerning His promise, as some count slackness, but is long suffering toward us, not willing that any should perish but that all should come to repentance" (2 Pet. 3:9).

In other words, the part of this world that makes up the Church has, as its main purpose, to collaborate with God so that together we may reach those who have not yet acknowledged Jesus Christ as their Lord and Savior.

THE GOD OF THIS AGE AND HIS STRATEGY

Many people who have not received Christ as their Lord and Savior have not done so because they *cannot*. They simply cannot because Satan has blinded them and holds them captive.

We complain many times about someone who, apparently, does not want to receive the gospel, without stopping to think that their lack of desire may not be the real reason. Any reasonable person to whom light is shown, will prefer light against darkness. But many cannot see the light.

We are often disdainful of a community, a region or a complete nation when we say, "They don't want to receive the gospel in that place!" We need to understand that the real problem is usually a spiritual one. The majority of people of many geographical regions are under the cover of darkness, which creates a veil over them. Paul refers to them as people, "Whose minds the god of this age has blinded, who do not believe, lest the light of the gospel of the glory of Christ, who is the image of God, should shine on them" (2 Cor. 4:4).

Evangelizing becomes difficult when our own attitude is negative. As Cindy Jacobs points out in this book, it can be a stronghold the enemy will use (see chapter 3). Cindy quotes Ed Silvoso's definition of a stronghold of the mind: "A mind set impregnated with hopelessness that causes the believer to accept as unchangeable something that he or she knows is contrary to the will of God." In our church in Guatemala we attempt to tear down this stronghold by operating under the principle: *no one is unreachable!*

Let me emphasize this principle. Although there may be exceptions, we assume that people we are witnessing to do not receive Christ because they *cannot*. Satan has "blinded their minds" according to 2 Corinthians 4:4. Our task, therefore, is to fight the spiritual battle on their behalf until the blindness is removed and the captives set free.

THE REALITY OF SPIRITUAL WARFARE

Spiritual warfare is the conflict between the Kingdom of Light and the kingdom of darkness, or Satan's kingdom. The two kingdoms are competing for the souls and spirits of the people who inhabit earth. This results in an ongoing battle involving two realms, the *visible* realm and the *invisible* realm. The spiritual battle that takes place in the heavenlies, in the invisible realm, is initiated in the hearts of people and has its final effect here on earth, in the visible realm. Those involved in this conflict are the following:

In the Kingdom of God:
1. God, the Father;
2. Jesus Christ;
3. The Holy Spirit;
4. The angels of God;
5. The church.

We find human beings at the center of this conflict. Lost humanity is the very reason for this battle. Unbelievers should be seen more on the side of the kingdom of darkness, because they are slaves of sin, and children of disobedience. Christ would say of them: "You are of your father the devil" (John 8:44). At the same time, we recognize that there is always a spiritual battle for believers who are already in the Kingdom of God. Even though believers are already in the Kingdom of God, they are still attacked by the devil who pursues the Church in order to stop the progress of God's plan.

On the other hand, the kingdom of darkness is made up of:
1. The devil;
2. The principalities;

3. The powers;
4. The rulers of darkness of this age;
5. The spiritual hosts of wickedness in the heavenly places;
6. And many other categories of dark angels named in Scripture, including power, might, dominion and every name that is named not only in this age but in that which is to come (see Eph. 1:21).

The Role of the Believer in the Conflict

Because of the knowledge we have from the Word, we understand that God has already done His part. He is certainly the major person of the Trinity in the Old Testament. In the New Testament, Jesus Christ is highlighted as personally defeating the devil on the cross of Calvary, and, "Having disarmed principalities and powers, He made a public spectacle of them, triumphing over them in it" (Col. 2:15).

The third person of the Trinity, the Holy Spirit is in our midst today for the purpose of guiding us, as the children of God. Even the angels of God who are attentive to His voice and are mighty in strength, in order to fulfill His word are waiting for the Church to make known the manifold wisdom of God to the principalities and powers in the heavenly places (see Eph. 3:10).

This, then, indicates that the Church has a key role. And the Church is *us!* Consequently, we can see an important part of our spiritual warfare as the effort put forth by the Church in order to remove the veil of blindness that has been placed by the devil on unbelievers.

We do two basic things: (1) We pierce the cover of darkness through strategic-level intercession, casting it down with the Word of God and the name of Jesus (Eph. 6:17,18). (2) We move in with evangelistic efforts (Eph. 6:15,19). We proclaim the Word of God in a way that people become exposed to the light of the gospel, which can now shine on them because the blindness has been removed. Many will accept Christ, who will then deliver them from the power of darkness and usher them into the Kingdom of the Son of His love.

THE NATURE OF SPIRITUAL WARFARE

For believers to perform their role in battle with integrity, they must clearly understand the following:

1. Spiritual warfare is not an end in itself. It is a powerful weapon that, when used as an integral part of evangelism, can increase the possibility of bringing others to Christ. Within this context, spiritual mapping is a strategic resource to locate the power of the enemy that hinders more fruitful evangelism.

2. Recognized characteristics of spiritual warfare are: (a) "We do not wrestle against flesh and blood, but against principalities, against powers, against the rulers of the darkness of this age, against spiritual hosts of wickedness in the heavenly places" (Eph. 6:12); and (b) "The weapons of our warfare are not carnal but mighty in God for pulling down strongholds" (2 Cor. 10:4).

3. A fact that, at times, seems to have been forgotten is the importance of persistence and steadfastness. The strategic level of spiritual warfare that deals with territorial spirits over complete cities and nations does not consist of an isolated skirmish, but of an outright war. This entails a constant succession of hostilities; not one battle, but multiple battles. The final outcome is certain: "Then comes the end, when He delivers the Kingdom to God the Father, when He puts an end to all rule and all authority and power" (1 Cor. 15:24).

Summarizing, we must understand that our human role in spiritual warfare is decisive and our involvement as prayer warriors is not optional, but indispensable in fulfilling God's Great Commission. Even Jesus Christ, when He describes His own ministry agenda in five facets, dedicates two of the facets to the theme of the need of liberating those who are being held captive. (See Luke 4:18,19.)

THE LINK BETWEEN THE SPIRITUAL AND EARTHLY REALMS

The interconnection between the invisible or spiritual realm and its counterpart, the visible or earthly realm, is an extremely important theme for us to understand. Each one of the spiritual kingdoms in the conflict has its own earthly counterpart.

None of us doubts the existence of an army representing the Kingdom of God, made up of angels, nor of the other well organized army of demons that serves the kingdom of darkness. Michael and his angels along with Satan and his angels are vividly described in Revelation 12. We need to know more of the ways these two armies relate to the men and women who serve their opposing kingdoms here on earth and how this affects our ultimate victory.

The Kingdom of Light has earthly servants of God who work to bear fruit for God. These servants are commonly divided into two subgroups: (1) Those called to full-time ministry (such as apostles, prophets, evangelists, pastors or teachers); and (2) the remaining brothers and sisters, members of the Body of Christ, called "ministers of the new covenant" (2 Cor. 3:6).

The first group is generally considered to be those on the frontlines of the battle. However, this first group would attain little without the constant aid and cooperation of the second group, which generally contributes most of the intercessors, those prayer warriors without whom victory would not be possible.

The kingdom of darkness also has its servants. In one group we have full-time ministers, who usually receive names such as warlocks, witches, shamans, sorcerers, channelers, satanic priests and priestesses, and so on. These, along with leaders of the cults and satanic sects, dedicate their lives to proclaim the deceits of the devil with the purpose of bringing people under captivity into their kingdom.

Right next to them is the group that causes us the most sadness. It is all those people who, because they have not yet received Christ, are still under the shroud of spiritual death and are manipulated to different degrees by the devil and his demons. These, in their ignorance, constitute the earthly army that the devil uses.

Knowing about the interaction taking place between the earthly army and the principalities and powers of the air will help guide us into victory. What could be better for an invading army than to know the enemy's position, to plot the location of their headquarters and to intercept their means of communication? This is precisely what spiritual mapping attempts to accomplish.

A REVEALING DREAM

A sister named Mirella, who attends our church, came up to me and said, "Pastor, I had a dream yesterday that made a great impression on me but I couldn't understand its meaning. This morning, while praying and asking God for the interpretation, He said to me: 'The dream is not for you. Go and tell it to the pastor since the dream is for him.'"

Needless to say, she caught my attention, but little did I imagine this was to be God's means to alter the way our church prays. It was to have far-reaching implications both for our church and our country.

The dream was the following: Mirella saw three cities of our country that she called by name, identifying them without any hesitation. Then she saw that a rope was uniting them—an invisible and transparent rope that she could see. A triangle took shape as the rope connected the three locations and three hands appeared, each holding one side. She said that the strange part was the hands. They were rough, almost rustic. They appeared to her like the hands of a strong man.

That was I all had to know.

Who Is the Strongman?

Days before this, I had been meditating considerably over the three synoptic references to the "strongman."

1. Matthew 12:29: "Or else how can one enter a strong man's house and plunder his goods, unless he first binds the strong man? And then he will plunder his house."
2. Mark 3:27: "No one can enter a strong man's house and plunder his goods, unless he first binds the strong man, and then he will plunder his house."
3. Luke 11:21,22: "When a strong man, fully armed, guards his own palace, his goods are in peace. But when a stronger than he comes upon him and overcomes him, he takes from him all his armor in which he trusted, and divides his spoils."

My interest was drawn to the word "man." Why was that word used so often in the Bible? Why strong *man*? Why not strong *spirit* or strong *principality* or strong *power*? Why did it have to be specifically "man"? I began to realize that God was speaking here of the interaction between human beings and the spiritual realm.

It is natural for all armies to have their leader, a captain or general who gives orders and decides what to do. That person could be called the *strongman* of the army. We know that some people have turned out to be extraordinarily wicked servants of Satan, such as Nero or Adolf Hitler. Both of them were powerful human tools for the evil one to do what he does best—steal, kill and destroy. We could accurately call them worldwide strongmen.

Hence, the devil chooses those who are willing to serve him and lifts them up as leaders on earth. It is obvious that a leader can influence many people and, therefore, can cause great destruction. These human leaders act as Satan's strongmen and they represent the characteristics of the principalities they serve. I believe that such strongmen on earth are assigned to principalities and powers in order to serve their purposes. These people cultivate an intimate and direct relationship with the demons through their occult activities.

We have the example of the relationship between the prince of Tyre and the king of Tyre in Ezekiel 28:2 and 12. Daniel gives us another example about the prince of Persia and the prince of Greece, who were obviously spiritual beings exerting direct relationship and influence over the empires of Persia and Greece through their emperors, their earthly rulers (see Dan. 10:20).

Isaiah 24:21 says, "So it will happen in that day, that the Lord will punish the host of heaven, on high, and the kings of the earth, on earth" *(NASB)*. Evidently the devil rules through kings of the earth. How? Undoubtedly through the intimate relationship of his dark angels with those people who choose to give themselves to Satan.

It is known that Adolf Hitler overtly participated in this process by inviting these powers of darkness to come inside him in order to make him the strongman of his time. It is also reported today that some contemporary world leaders belong to cults of the New Age or to secret societies that seek to rule the world.

The Relationship Between the
Spiritual Kingdom and Humanity

God wants to bless people. He calls people and they respond by dedicating their lives to serve Him. They become His servants and depend totally on Him. They weave communication lines with Him, such as prayer, worship and listening to the Father. We all acknowledge as fact the following principle: The more intimate the communication with God, the greater the anointing and the more success in Christian ministry.

It seems that the devil, who copies and corrupts everything he can, also has servants who have chosen him as their lord and have dedicated their lives to serve him. They, too, have lines of communication with their lord through things such as witchcraft, sorcery, sacrifices, seances, transcendental meditation and covenants. They also operate under the same principle: The more intimate the communication, the greater the power. When I realized this, I began to see that God was revealing to us the names of the strongmen in Guatemala so that we could recognize, through them, the ruling principalities. God was revealing the enemy to us, not to glorify the enemy, but to help us defeat him.

Binding Strongmen in Guatemala

As a consequence of Mirella's dream, I had a conversation with a brother in our church who has a prophetic ministry. As he heard the dream, he answered immediately: "Do you know who the three persons in the three cities are?" He proceeded to give me their first and last names! Upon doing some research, we confirmed that these three men all secretly conducted evil works of the devil in their three cities. One of them had power through money, the second one through politics, and the third one through drug dealing.

God gave us a strategy right at that point. He said: "You bind those principalities in the name of Jesus. You pluck up, break down, destroy and overthrow the lines of communication that give power to these strongmen and do not curse the individuals involved, but bless them, because they were made in the image and likeness of God."

Obviously, I cannot reveal their names, but I can say that, as a direct consequence of *on-site* prayer, the first one has lost all his power and is in jail waiting to be judged for his crimes. The second one is about to be impeached and thrown out of office, and the third one, at a critical time in his political career, suffered personal problems and has now lost most of his influence and power. The strongmen were cast down at the same time that the powers in the heavenlies were being bound and overthrown by the prayers of the saints.

In this case, spiritual warfare brought forth fruit, not only spiritually, but also naturally, and the result has been a scriptural one. Having bound and defeated the strongman, we could then proceed to take from him all his armor in which he trusted, and divide his spoils. In this case, the spoils have been more fruitful evangelism, peace, reduction of violence, and the change of the spiritual government from darkness to light. Guatemala now has a Christian president, Jorge Serrano, who is filled with the Holy Spirit, and who also happens to be a member of our church.

To summarize, we have learned that it is to our advantage to know who the strongman is in order to bind him and divide his spoils. Spiritual mapping helps us identify the strongman. In some cases, spiritual mapping will give us a series of characteristics that will guide us directly to the territorial prince or power. In other cases, we will find ourselves facing a natural person whom Satan is using. In still others, we will find ourselves face-to-face with a corrupt social structure.

Spiritual Mapping in the Field

After understanding the importance of attempting to discern

each power over particular regions by name, we went out to do our first field experiment. In November 1990, small groups of people were sent by the church to the capital cities of each of the 22 departments of Guatemala (or counties) to fast, pray and seek the guidance of the Lord to identify the principality over each department. In His mercy, God permitted us to have

---

Mature spiritual mapping requires coordinated effort aimed at taking each territory. Our purpose is to do spiritual warfare to open the door for effective evangelism and positive social change.

---

extraordinary results and we saw, for the first time, a sort of spiritual X ray, a true spiritual map of the situation in the heavenlies over our country. Our spiritual warfare became much more effective and we could see physical results of our spiritual effort much more abundantly than we had previously imagined.

Our leaders felt sure that this was a viable approach for a local church to evangelize the geographical area in which it is located. We therefore persevered until we developed a working model. We are now using this model in the micro-mapping of neighborhoods and subdivisions before we evangelize and plant churches there.

PRACTICAL INSTRUCTIONS FOR SPIRITUAL MAPPING

Mature spiritual mapping requires coordinated effort aimed at taking each territory. Our purpose is to do spiritual warfare to open the door for effective evangelism and positive social change.

THE MASTER PLAN

A. Vision:
Evangelization of the nation

B. Specific objectives:
1. To enter into spiritual warfare with the purpose of fighting spiritually for our nation until we are victorious.
2. To do spiritual mapping that enables us to know so far as possible the enemy's plans, strategies and plots in order to go into battle with intelligence and, as a result, be victorious within a minimum of time, and with a minimum of risk and loss.
3. If done well, the spiritual victory will result in affecting the nation through revival, reform and social justice, all of which are caused by the free moving of the Holy Spirit in the country.

C. Procedure:
The procedure involves dividing the battlefield into geographical territories, which are all worked simultaneously.

1. Define each territory with precision.
2. Secure the work team and its leaders.
3. Do spiritual mapping according to the manual.
4. Discern the enemy's situation over the assigned territory.
5. Evaluate, arrange and communicate the information needed for spiritual warfare.

A MANUAL FOR SPIRITUAL MAPPING

To do the job, we divide ourselves into three teams, each one being assigned to one of three areas of research. The teams are not allowed to communicate with each other. This provides us with an information cross-check from each of the three areas, enabling us to receive confirmation, which adds credibility to our results.

The three working teams are assigned respectively to research historical factors, physical factors and spiritual factors.

HISTORICAL FACTORS

To do the historical research, we must ask the following questions in each city or neighborhood:

1. The name or names

We must make a list or inventory of the names used for our territory and then ask ourselves the following questions:

- Does the name have a meaning?
- If the etymological name has no meaning, does it have any implication at all?
- Is it a blessing or a curse?
- Is it a native, Indian or foreign name?
- Does it say anything at all about the first inhabitants of that land?
- Does it describe any characteristics of the people who live there?
- Is there any relation between the name and the attitude of its inhabitants?
- Do any of these names have a direct relation to the names of demons or the occult?

- Is the name linked to any religion, belief or local cult of the place?

2. Nature of the territory

- Does this territory have any special characteristics that distinguishes it from others?
- Is it closed or open to evangelism?
- Are there many or few churches?
- Is evangelization easy or hard?
- Is the socioeconomic condition of the territory uniform? Are there drastic changes?
- List the most common social problems of the neighborhood, such as drug addiction, alcoholism, abandoned families, corruption of the environment, greed, unemployment, exploitation of the poor, etc.
- Is there any specific area that draws our attention? For example, could we define this territory or its inhabitants with one word? What would it be?

3. History of the territory

For this job we turn to interviews, research in city hall, in the libraries, etc. An extremely important issue here is to know which events give a clue to the birth of this neighborhood or territory and under what circumstances this took place.

- When did it originate?
- Who was its founder (or founders)?
- What was the original purpose for its foundation?
- What can we learn from the founder? The founder's religion, beliefs, habits? Were some idol-worshipers?
- Are there events that have happened frequently such as deaths, violence, tragedies or accidents?

(Such as the so-called "death corner" we have in our city.)
- Is there any factor that suggests the presence of a curse or of a territorial spirit?
- Are there frightening stories? Are they valid? What caused them?
- How far back does the history of the Christian church go in this place?
- How did it start? Was it the fruit of a specific factor?

This list of questions is not by any means exhaustive, but it is a beginning. We must not forget the Holy Spirit will be our main helper in this.

PHYSICAL FACTORS

The physical aspect refers to significant material objects we might find in our territory. It seems that the devil, due to his unlimited pride, frequently leaves a trail behind. So it is necessary to:

- Do an intensive study of the maps available for this region, including the oldest maps and the newest maps, which allow us to identify changes. Do the streets have a particular order? Do they suggest any kind of drawing or pattern?
- Make an inventory of parks.
- Make an inventory of monuments.
- Are there archaeological sites in our territory?
- Make an inventory of statues and study their characteristics.
- What type of institutions stand out in our territory? Power institutions, social institutions, religious institutions or others?

- How many churches do we have in the territory?
- Make an inventory of the places where God is worshiped and the places where the devil is worshiped.
- An extremely important question is: Are there "high places" in our territory?
- Are there excessive numbers of bars or witchcraft centers or abortion clinics, or porno shops?
- A thorough study of the demographics will be of great help.
- Study the socioeconomic conditions of the neighborhood, crimes, violence, injustice, pride, blessings and curses.
- Are there cult centers in the community? Does their location have any specific distribution?

In Guatemala we have a 50-kilometer road that goes to the city of Antigua, Guatemala, and along this road we have seen all sorts of cults flourish in a straight line, including: Baha'i, Jehovah's Witnesses, Islam, New Age, witch doctors, and so on. A road like this undoubtedly constitutes an occult line of power, a corridor through which demons and the demonic powers move. These occult power lines come from contamination brought to earth by the devil through curses and invocations of territorial spirits that we are now discovering. It is helpful to locate them in order to reverse the curse and make them blessings.

SPIRITUAL FACTORS

Spiritual factors can be the most important factors of all, because they reveal the real cause behind the symptoms exposed through the historical and physical research.

Those called to work in this spiritual area are the intercessors, people who flow in the gift of discernment of spirits and accurately hear from God. The group of intercessors must turn to intense prayer with the purpose of knowing the mind of Christ and receiving from God the description of the spiritual status of the enemy in the heavenly places over the defined territory.

We also have some questions the intercessors need to ask that will help guide our prayers, but they cannot be a substitute for spending quality time with God on behalf of the place for which we are praying.

- Are the heavens open in this place?
- Is it easy to pray in this place? Or is there much oppression?
- Can we discern a cover of darkness? Can we define its territorial dimension?
- Are there express differences in the spiritual atmosphere over the regions of our territory? In other words, are the heavenly places more open or closed over different subdivisions, neighborhoods or communities in the area? Can we determine with accuracy these separations?
- Has God revealed a name to us?
- Does the information we have reveal a power or principality we can recognize?
- Has God shown us the "strongman"?

We might become discouraged by seeing all of these questions in writing, but if we confide in the work of the Holy Spirit and God's desire to reveal His secrets, we will feel confident. This is not a job requiring mystical people, nor is it something weird. All we need is a work team that feels a true burden for evangelism in a specific territory, and the rest is the guidance of the Holy Spirit.

When we have completed the research on all three factors, we turn it over to a mature group of leaders and intercessors to evaluate the information. Bev Klopp provides an example of this in chapter 8. We have found that research on each of the three factors will confirm and complement the work of the other two if we are accurately hearing what the Spirit is saying to us.

NAMING THE STRONGMAN

We have had truly exciting experiences. For example, one day God showed the historical factors team an area where there were archaeological remains and how they related to basic characteristics of idolatry and witchcraft dating back to the Mayan civilization. Those of the physical factors team simultaneously located a vacant house in exactly the same area where idolatry and witchcraft meetings were taking place. Afterward, God showed the intercessors of the spiritual factors team that the territorial spirit ruling over that place was using a human being as the strongman. His life-style included practicing the occult, witchcraft and idolatry.

While we were in prayer the Lord spoke and said, "Tomorrow I will give you the man's first and last name in the newspaper." He also told us on which page it would appear. It was something absolutely supernatural and exciting to discover right on that page the full name of the person dedicated to these activities. He fit the exact description the Holy Spirit had previously given, even down to his physical appearance. To cap it off, we discovered that this man was also the owner of the vacant house where the occult rituals were taking place, right across the street from the archaeological site!

Once we have come to such conclusions, we are ready to do spiritual warfare. We must remember that our battle is not against flesh and blood, but against the demonic powers that rule over people. Also, we must remember we are called to bless the people involved, not to curse them. Lastly, we remember that Christ Jesus has already won the battle for us!

CONCLUSION

Territoriality of spirits is a fact as far as we in our church are concerned. We have studied the subject in the Scriptures. We have done our homework in the field. We understand that the evil army of heaven demands worship and service from its followers and bestows evil power in proportion to their obedience.

When a territory has been inhabited by persons who have chosen to offer their worship to demons, the land has been contaminated and those territorial spirits have obtained a right to remain there, keeping the inhabitants captive. It is then necessary to identify the enemy and to go into spiritual battle, until we obtain victory and redeem the territory. Spiritual mapping is a means toward identifying the enemy. It is our spiritual espionage.

We have no time to lose! Now is the time for the Body of Christ to rise in the power of the Holy Spirit and challenge the powers of hell, destroying all its schemes and taking back the land the Lord God has given to us as an inheritance.

■■ REFLECTION QUESTIONS ■■

1. Harold Caballeros focuses on winning the lost to Christ—evangelism. How does he see spiritual mapping as a means toward more effective evangelism?

2. The concept that many unbelievers do not accept Christ because they *cannot* is new to some of us. We usually think

it is because they do not *want to*. What is your opinion on this issue?

3. Is there any possible direct relationship between a spiritual "strongman" and a living person? Can you think of any examples in your city or nation?

4. What is the historical origin of your city's name? Why was this name chosen? Does any feature of your city today seem to reflect what is behind the name?

5. Think of your city or town. Try to name at least three internal geographical areas that are clearly different from each other. Describe the visible characteristics and try to suggest what may be the invisible or spiritual powers behind each area.

Practical Steps Toward Community Deliverance

by Bob Beckett

B OB BECKETT IS THE FOUNDING PASTOR OF THE DWELLING
Place Family Church in Hemet, California. He
began spiritually mapping his community in the
1970s and is now helping to coordinate Christian leaders in Southern California for extensive mapping projects. Bob is a member of the Spiritual Warfare Network
and is in wide demand as a speaker on the subject of
spiritual warfare.

In 1974, my wife Susan and I were asked to become
directors for a minimum security juvenile facility owned
by a large church based in Orange County, California.

The 360-acre facility was located in a remote community called San Jacinto in the desert southwest of Palm Springs.

I will never forget wondering why the Lord would move us into the middle of nowhere. After all, I somewhat haughtily thought the Lord had called me to minister His Word and stand against darkness in some place of significance. Instead, here I was living in a remote retirement community almost as far from anything seemingly important or crucial to the Kingdom of God as one could get! At least this is how San Jacinto appeared to us in the natural. Little did I know at the time that I had moved into a stronghold of darkness for a major portion of the Southern California Inland Empire!

THE NAVEL OF THE EARTH?

Shortly after arriving on the facility we were to call home for the next three years, I learned from the former owner that the property had previously been used as a metaphysical retreat and training center for Transcendental Meditation. During one of our first conversations, the former owner asked if I would be interested in visiting one of the "navels of the earth." At the time I was not sure I knew what he meant. But curiosity had a good grip on me, so off we went.

We proceeded to hike up a now dry streambed to a remote corner of the property nestled against the foothills. Along the way, he began to tell me how this was a very sacred location to those who were spiritually in tune with "the cosmos."

We finally stopped at the location of what was once the sight of a waterfall that had flowed year round. He carefully pointed out how the walls of the canyon had been scarred over the centuries by the water as it fell in a circular motion. He went on to explain that this location was a "navel" or vortex of the earth, a useful power center in training persons desiring to engage in upper levels of Transcendental Meditation.

One of their highest spiritual exercises for those at the TM retreat center would be to go to the waterfall any time the rains would fill the canyon. They would meditate at the vortex of the waterfall until the water no longer swirled in a clockwise motion, as water naturally does above the equator, but in reverse of its natural course. The waterfall was a key part of their training facility. My guide went on to point out that the walls of the canyon had been scarred over time in a clockwise motion, but the sand and earth of the dry streambed had clearly been marked in a counterclockwise motion.

All this was intriguing and mysterious, but I had a juvenile facility on my mind. I was not ready to debate the validity of all this and how it would ever relate to me. I must admit, however, that some time after our encounter I was puzzled why he felt so strongly about sharing all this with me. I now believe it was the Lord slowly nudging me in a direction I would never have gone on my own.

THREE POWER POINTS ON THE MAP

One day, not too long after my conversation with the previous owner, I was planning to hunt in our area. While browsing over a map, I casually marked down the location of the navel. I was interested to see that our property and the navel were adjacent to the local Indian reservation, which was reported to be active in traditional Indian shamanism.

Not long after this, a rumor began to circulate in town that Maharishi Yogi had purchased property in our community. I happened to notice that the rumored location was also adjacent to the local Indian reservation. Curiosity began to grip me now. Why would he purchase property in this quiet little community? On one occasion I spoke with someone who was working on the newly acquired property. When I asked him why the Yogi had chosen this specific location for his retreat facility, he said, "This area is very conducive to meditation and has a spiritual aura about it."

Though at the time I did not give a great deal of credence to such claims, I felt impressed also to mark this location on the same map. My map now showed three reported locations of spiritual activity: the navel, the Indian reservation and Maharishi Yogi's property, all adjacent to one another.

A Bearhide with a Backbone

In my times of personal prayer, I began to have a recurring vision that would flash before me. It looked something like a bearhide laying on the floor. Each of the four corners of the hide was that of a leg area with the claws attached. The hide had no head, but appeared to have a backbone. Each time I would see this animal's hide it would be centered over our local mountain area. Each set of claws in the vision was embedded in specific locations, including the Hemet/San Jacinto valley. All the other cities were within a 30-mile radius of our community.

I should mention that I would never see this in a dream. It was always while I was awake and almost always in times of prayer. Each time I would see this vision I vaguely felt it could have something to do with ruling spirits of darkness such as those referred to in Daniel 10, namely the prince of Persia and the prince of Greece.

During one prayer time, I felt strongly impressed to take a group of 12 church leaders to a specific cabin located in the mountains covered by this vision. By this time, Susan and I were pastoring a small church we had planted in the small city of Hemet. As I approached the elders and several other seasoned leaders in our congregation with my sense of direction from the Lord, they agreed to go with me to the cabin, which belonged to a woman in our church. We were to pray there until we broke the "backbone" of this ruling spirit and forced it to loose its spiritual grip upon the people living under its control.

God greatly encouraged me when I approached the woman who owned the cabin. I entered the store in town that she operated. When she saw me, she reached down behind the counter and tossed the keys of the cabin to me. Then she said, "In my prayer time this morning God told me you would come and I was to give you the keys!"

As we all gathered in the cabin the following Friday, I explained in detail this recurring vision and what I felt our purpose was on this mountain. I shared with the group that I thought we would all know when we had broken the back of this thing by hearing or feeling the breaking. After hours of praying and agonizing and ministering to the Lord, we spontaneously began to sing, "There Is Power in the Blood." Each of us had been alerted by an immediate and gripping sense of evil all around us. While singing that song we all felt it break! Many of us even heard an audible sound as if vertebrae were not exactly cracking, but popping or disjointing. The whole cabin physically shook!

A deep sense of relief came upon all of us as we drove down the mountain the next day. We did not understand exactly what we had done, nor what to expect as a result of our time together. Things, however, began to happen spiritually in our seemingly dull and sleepy little retirement community. We all sensed that something was different in our town.

THE LONESOME GODS

Many years later Peter and Doris Wagner came to visit, along with our old friends Cindy and Mike Jacobs. Up to that point, I had kept the well-worn map I had been making confidential. I had added several other power points including the huge, opulent, and well-fortified Church of Scientology Media Center and resort, which L. Ron Hubbard built. I had never said much about my map, because few in the Christian community had been talking about such things and I did not want to appear as if I were on the lunatic fringe. But Cindy encouraged me to show it to Peter and Doris, which I did with trepidation. Displaying such a thing to a seminary professor was somewhat intimidating.

I was greatly encouraged when I received total affirmation. Peter said that his contacts through the Spiritual Warfare Network had confirmed that doing such spiritual mapping was one of the strong new words the Holy Spirit seemed to be giving to the churches all over the world these days. He then confessed he was an avid reader of Louis L'Amour's frontier novels and asked me if I had read *The Lonesome Gods* (Bantam Books). He said the setting was located here in the San Jacinto region and it dealt with the early Indian legends. The next week I bought the book and read it. I was intrigued by the clear description of *Taquitz*, the ruling spirit of the San Jacinto mountain range.

You can imagine my amazement when I researched this further and discovered that the huge rock right behind the cabin in which we had prayed to break the backbone was none other than what was called Taquitz Peak!

DISCOVERING OUR COMMUNITY'S SPIRITUAL HERITAGE

I had kept the map to myself for 17 years, marking what I thought might be of some importance. During this same time, I became very interested in knowing more of the history of our community and its founding fathers. Often I would spend my days off hiking into remote areas and unexplored canyons, investigating caves and looking for old cabins and Indian relics.

One canyon, known as Massacre Canyon, was the sight of the slaughter of the Soboba Indian tribe by another neighboring tribe, the Temeculas. Having some understanding of the scriptural basis for land defilement, I began to wonder if this incident and its location had any spiritual significance. I dutifully marked Massacre Canyon on my map.

Another important past event in the life of our community was an attempt by a local water company to drill a major water line through the foothills on the north side of our valley. This proved to be very significant. The water company miscalculated their drilling and tapped into the underground water table nourishing the whole area!

For 18 months water flowed unchecked. All efforts to stop the flow of water resulted in disastrous consequences. The cost was great, not only financially, but also in the loss of human life. Eventually, the water table for the entire valley and surrounding mountains deteriorated. The area would never be the same.

This explained why I would find abandoned citrus and poultry ranches high upon the hillsides on numerous excursions into the foothills. They seemingly flourished prior to the water drilling disaster. All had irrigation systems and large holding ponds for water, diverted from the streams that once flowed year-round. But after the drilling disaster, even the local Indian reservation had lost its abundant water supply and its agricultural base, sending the inhabitants into poverty.

Many on the reservation today can still recall how infuriated the tribal council became over this. Their shamans cursed the white man's water company for the error. Matters were made worse when rumor had it that the water company was deliberately diverting the water and selling it to other water companies, secretly making no real attempt to stop the water flow, much less to compensate the Indians for their losses.

After locating the sight of the drilling on my map, I noticed it fell along the same range of foothills where the navel of the earth, the Indian reservation, Maharishi Yogi and the site of the Indian massacre were located! I knew this was somehow significant, but I was still unsure what to do with such information. So I continued to mark my map with findings I felt were affecting the spiritual heritage of our community.

At that same time, L. Ron Hubbard and the Church of Scientology moved into town. They had purchased on old country club located on a specific piece of property along the same range of foothills as the Massacre Canyon, the water line disaster, Yogi, the reservation and the navel. As a matter of fact, the place they purchased was called Massacre Canyon Inn. Something was going on in this area and my map was beginning to make it very obvious. If I had not seen these things on a map I would probably never have made any association between these locations. But seeing them plotted on a map gave it all a coherent perspective.

UNANSWERED PRAYER FOR THE COMMUNITY

As I mentioned, I remained silent about the map and my suspicions, even though our congregation by this time was deeply committed to prayer and intercession early every weekday morning. In our church, The Dwelling Place Church, we would pray briefly over one need after another, hitting international and national issues as well as praying over individuals and community needs for our area. But all along there was a deep sense of frustration building in all of us who stood faithfully in prayer for our people and our community. This frustration came from a growing realization that in all honesty our prayers had not been very effective.

We had learned to pray effectively for people and we were seeing men and women freed from emotional, spiritual, financial and physical bondage. Many had been saved in The Dwelling Place Church because they had seen God's power in physical healing or had been delivered from demonic oppression.

Why were similar things not happening in our community?

Why could it be that our prayers for people were answered but our prayers for Hemet and the surrounding area seemed ineffective? We looked to the north, the south, the east and the west from our church and saw little change. It seemed as if in some aspects our community was losing ground. Social conditions were deteriorating and we could sense encroaching darkness. We felt we were being faithful and diligent, but to little avail.

As I agonized over this, I began mentally to walk through the approach we used for freeing people from demonic bondage. Would it be possible to apply these same principles in the social realm just as we do in the personal realm? Could it be that cities have a personality?

This led me to dig into the Scriptures and seek a biblical base for the concept of a city having a personality. If this premise turned out to be biblically valid, new steps might be taken to see our community *as a community*, not simply as people, delivered and set free.

Evil spirits, I knew, seek to control a personality or character. They find their entrance into a person's life through past sins, current sins, generational curses and iniquities, idolatry, victimization, trauma, forms of personal defilement and so forth. When a person's personality is defiled, the door is then opened to darkness in that personality, because Satan dwells in darkness. My search to confirm a city's personality led me to Jesus' comments in Matthew 11:20-24:

> Then He began to upbraid the cities in which most of His mighty works had been done, because they did not repent: "Woe to you, Chorazin! Woe to you, Bethsaida! For if the mighty works which were done in you had been done in Tyre and Sidon, they would have repented long ago in sackcloth and ashes. But I say to you, it will be more tolerable for Tyre and Sidon in the day of judgment than for you. And you, Capernaum,

who are exalted to heaven, will be brought down to
Hades; for if the mighty works which were done in
you had been done in Sodom, it would have remained
until this day. But I say to you that it shall be more tol-
erable for the land of Sodom in the day of judgment
than for you."

Here it is clear that Jesus is referring to a city's personal
responsibility. Each city, it appears, is addressed as a personality having responsibility for its actions and its response to the
gospel. Of course, Jesus is not saying that a city has an eternal
soul, but He does refer to cities as corporate entities. He
addresses each one directly by name.

Still desiring more biblical confirmation I searched the Word,
studying cities and looking for any information that might lead
me to uncover more truth in this area. Hebrews 11:10 says,
"For he [Abraham] waited for the city which has foundations,
whose builder and maker is God." Abraham was looking for a
city that had incorporated godly principles into its very foundation. The Greek word for "foundation" can also be translated
"rudimentary principles and precepts." This speaks of a city's
morals and ethics. So built within every city's walls is its character and personality!

I also discovered that this Greek word for foundation is the
very same word Paul uses in 1 Corinthians 3:11,12 as he
instructs the church regarding the foundation of human personality: "For no other foundation can anyone lay than that
which is laid, which is Jesus Christ. Now if anyone builds on this
foundation with gold, silver, precious stones, wood, hay, straw."

We began wondering what the foundations of our own city
could have been built upon. Was it Jesus Christ? Is our community built with gold, silver and precious stones, or does it
have some wood, hay and stubble? Sadly, we saw much wood,
hay and stubble in the Hemet area.

COMMUNICATING WITH THE CITY

I began to believe that ministering deliverance to a city might indeed be possible. My community, as well as your community, can be thought of as having its own personality with very real spiritual foundations! A key would be to communicate with the city and, of course, this presents us with a unique challenge. How can we get our city to "speak" back to us as a person would? How can we get it to tell us about the things that have happened to its land? How has it been defiled and opened up to territorial spirits? Just how could I get my city to open up and talk to me?

Again, after prayer and searching the Word of God for answers I found a hint. "Call to Me and I will answer you and show you great and mighty things, *fenced in and hidden*, which you do not know—do not distinguish and recognize, have knowledge of and understand" (Jer. 33:3, *AMP*, emphasis mine). This verse indicated that the hidden and unseen things, which I could not understand, could be important to the Lord. As we seek Him in prayer over these hidden things, we believe He is faithful and will answer us and show us these hidden truths. The Lord indicated that a key to dealing with the community would be to ask the same questions we would of a person seeking freedom from demonic oppression, and that He would lead us in the specifics of actually setting our city on the road to deliverance.

We now needed to find out how our city's spiritual foundations had been laid. What were the foundations made of? Where were the aches and pains located? What were the events that led up to bondage in the city? How does past history relate to current happenings? Is there occult involvement in my city? Has anything else played a role in leading up to my city's current spiritual, emotional or physical condition?

Little did I realize I had already been communicating with

my city for nearly 19 years! A way to communicate or talk with a city is to study and research the city's history and heritage.

Could my mapping and historical knowledge of my city somehow be linked together to speak to me about the city's foundation—good and bad? As I began to pour through this information once again, I gradually began to see my community's spiritual personality emerge. It was somewhat like taking a jigsaw puzzle out of a box, dumping it all out on a table and watching piece after piece fall into place.

SCUD MISSILES AND SMART BOMBS

Suddenly I found myself looking at a picture of my city's personality as I had never seen it before. It was exciting to think we would now be able to minister deliverance and initiate the process that might bring spiritual freedom to our valley. Could this also be the missing element that our prayer and intercession was so desperately in need of? Had we really been hitting our targets in prayer or were we actually just praying around the need in a vague and ineffective way.

I thought of the Scud missiles Saddam Hussein launched during the 1991 Gulf War. Even though these missiles were aimed in the right direction, and they did strike some vague targets, their obvious lack of accuracy prevented the missiles from achieving their full destructive potential. I began to see that our prayer for our community was somewhat like the dictator's misguided missiles. We were striking out at the enemy but because of our lack of strategic information, we were incapable of isolating or discerning a specific target, aiming at it and hitting it.

Now that we were beginning to accumulate strategic information on our city's personality (e.g., its heritage, foundation, spiritual background), we were able to form a strategic war plan and to strike precise targets. This was much like the smart bombs the allies aimed back at Saddam Hussein. Those of us who watched TV were amazed as these smart bombs were directed into specific doors, windows and air vents of buildings.

But for any spiritual smart bombs to be that precise, someone must first gather reconnaissance information. An exploration of the area must first be done. For us, this means doing research, studying the land and the primary settlers, mapping and digging into the history of our city. Spiritual warfare, like conventional warfare, benefits greatly from accurate intelligence.

Spiritual mapping has proved to be an effective tool for strategic intercession and strategic acts of intercession for our community. As I sat back and reviewed my years of information gathering, I realized I had intuitively plotted significant parts of my area's history onto my map. There, in front of me, was historical, physical and spiritual information. Little had I realized the significance this map would have in the years to come.

This worn map proved to be invaluable in forming a strategy against territorial strongholds and spirits that had lodged themselves into our community. Once we, as a congregation, learned to communicate with our city's "personality," the results of our intercession escalated dramatically.

MAPPING A CITY
What then are the necessary steps for a pastor, lay person or congregation to begin spiritual mapping?

The City's History
First, research the history and the foundation of the community. Look for points of defilement, such as bloodshed, broken contracts, broken covenants and racial prejudices that may have old city laws attached to them, which still remain on the books at city hall.

I had staff pouring over local history books, visiting museums and sitting in our local library going through city documents. One of the interesting things we discovered was an old historical landmark located on the property of a local church in the community. This was a large archway the county had preserved and declared a historical landmark because one of the first high schools in the county had been built there.

The pastor of that local church is a close personal friend and we had both become very interested in the history of his church property and its possible relationship to this landmark. His research had uncovered some interesting information. His church and the historical landmark were located precisely on the site of the village of the Soboba Indians who, as I mentioned before, were massacred by the neighboring Temeculas. They began the slaughter in what is now San Jacinto and, as the warriors were fighting, the women and children fled from this village to Massacre Canyon where later they all met their death.

Our research went on to reveal that since the church was founded in the early 1900s, every single pastor or pastor's family member had experienced a violent death, with the exception of the present pastor and the pastor prior to him. We could not help but wonder if the violence and bloodshed in the past had defiled that piece of land and given a foothold for a spirit of violent death to operate. We also thought this might help explain why that particular neighborhood had become the geographical center for gang violence in the whole area.

When the pastor learned about the Indian bloodshed and the history of violent deaths among pastors, he called a meeting of his elders and intercessors. They engaged in a time of sincere intercession and deep repentance for their land and their church.

What happened? Less than two months later, gang members began to come to the Lord. At least one walked into the church during the Sunday service and said, "I want to be saved!" Another gang leader, his mother, and then the entire family came to Christ. Gang violence in the area has dropped since then, although it has not yet disappeared entirely.

The City's Personality

The second step we took in the spiritual mapping of our community was to research the formation of our city's personality. In other words, what was our city known for? Las Vegas is known for greed and gambling; Chicago for mob violence and San Francisco for its gay and lesbian strongholds. Our own community is known as a retirement community, a place where older people come to spend their last days in ease and then die.

In this second step of mapping, we searched out financial

A vital area not to be overlooked in our desire to see our community freed from spiritual bondage is that of repentance and remitting the sins of communities.

---

institutions and any businesses or buildings the city seemed to cluster around. We discovered that Hemet has the largest amounts of bank deposits per capita of any city in the United States. We located bars, pornographic theaters and drug centers.

The City's Cult Centers

The third step of our mapping process was to search out psychic, occult, New Age, metaphysical, holistic and cult centers. We took note of shrines, Mormon temples, New Age book stores and all churches and properties operated by cults. Along with this third step we searched out occult activity. We talked to high school kids involved in drugs and satanism and we interviewed descendants of local Indian witch doctors. Many times vacant and abandoned houses are used for animal sacrifices and rituals, so these were checked out as well.

REPENTING FOR SOCIAL SINS

We were to learn that another vital area not to be overlooked in our desire to see our community freed from spiritual bondage was that of repentance and remitting the sins of communities. This topic is covered in more detail in John Dawson's book *Taking Our Cities for God*[1] and in Cindy Jacob's book *Possessing the Gates of the Enemy*.[2] In September 1991, Peter Wagner and Cindy Jacobs spoke during our church's Strategic Warfare Conference. At the conference we were able to put into practice this concept of repentance over our city, seeking God's forgiveness for social sins.

Upon Cindy's coaching, local Indians and a representative of the water company came together in front of the conference and publicly repented to each other for the misdeeds of the past. A local Methodist pastor stood on the platform with a Pentecostal pastor and each apologized for pride and divisiveness between evangelicals and charismatics. Finally, a white man and an Indian stood face-to-face and repented over sins and hatred between the two races. As each of these repented one at a time, forgave each other, and then openly embraced each other, many in the conference wept aloud as years of division and hatred were broken in the spiritual realm. The principalities and powers received serious setbacks that evening.

PASTORAL COMMITMENT TO A TERRITORY

During my early days of prayer for my community and its people, I felt the Lord begin to stir within me a strong love for the land and its people. I had never seen myself anchored to this community. I always hoped in my heart that someday I would be off somewhere with a worldwide ministry of some sort. But the Lord began to show me that I could never begin to bring deliverance of any real and lasting significance to my own area if I was living here with my emotional and spiritual bags packed, always waiting for the day when the Lord would call me to a larger community with greater influence and significance.

Yet that is the very thing I was doing; I was always waiting for that "higher call!" I realized that what I lacked was a *territorial commitment.* I feel that this turned out to be a key element toward initiating the deliverance of my city.

If my city would ever know true deliverance from its ruling spirits of religious apathy, financial stinginess, occult idolatry and the like, it would have to start with Christian leaders making a commitment to the people and the land. Someone like me needed to begin by unpacking their bags and setting aside their dream of a more exciting ministry in the future. Pastors, lay leaders and whole churches must join, taking long-term territorial responsibility for the land they are living in! Susan and I began by announcing to our congregation that we considered Hemet a lifetime call and by purchasing our cemetery plots.

A passage in Jeremiah speaks of a time when Israel's leaders ignored their responsibilities. "Many rulers have destroyed My vineyard, they have trodden My portion under foot; they have made My pleasant portion a desolate wilderness. They have made it desolate; desolate, *it mourns to Me;* the whole land is made desolate, because *no one takes it to heart"* (Jer. 12:10,11, emphasis mine).

Our church began as never before to take our land to heart. One Sunday morning I felt the prompting of the Holy Spirit to take our whole congregation up on the side of a hill that overlooks the entire Hemet/San Jacinto valley. There we stood elbow to elbow, hands extended toward Hemet, for half an hour and interceded against the spiritual darkness that gripped our community.

One year my wife Susan felt the Lord instruct our church to enter the annual Hemet Christmas parade. We again dutifully obeyed, entered the parade, and marched down the main street of our city singing praises to Jesus with songs such as, "What a Mighty God We Serve" and "Make a Joyful Noise Unto the Lord."

Last year our church entry had more than 450 people from our congregation participating in song, choreographed dance, flag carrying, banner holding and float sitting. We endeavored to minister to the people in our community through our entry,

---

I am convinced that when we learn to embrace our territorial commitment and assigned sphere of influence, and as we learn how to destroy strongholds and ruling principalities and powers over our communities, we will, city by city, begin to incorporate ourselves into God's final plan for our cities and nations.

---

and at the same time make a strong statement to the spirits of darkness. The response from the community has been tremendous; many people are committing themselves back into local churches and businesses are now donating money and materials to help us defray the cost of our entry. Last year the judges of the Christmas parade were also impressed and awarded our church entry the highest award—the Presidential Trophy. I share this not out of personal pride, but to show how an average congregation can really love a city and "take it to heart" as mentioned in Jeremiah.

I am convinced that when we learn to embrace our territorial commitment and assigned sphere of influence, and as we learn how to destroy strongholds and ruling principalities and powers over our communities, we will, city by city, begin to incorporate ourselves into God's final plan for our cities and nations.

STAKING OUR CITY FOR GOD

Recently while praying about the increasing gang violence in our community, we felt the need to establish a prayer canopy over our city. We had prayed for a spiritual covering over our city previously but had never done anything quite as tangible as we felt the Lord leading us to do.

In prayer, I was drawn to Isaiah 33:20-23, a passage I had read many times, never feeling that this prophecy to Assyria had any direct connection with my ministry. This time I felt, however, that God wanted me to pay attention to the literal text and apply it to taking our city for God. It is important to have the Scripture before us as I explain:

> Look upon Zion, the city of our appointed feasts;
> Your eyes will see Jerusalem, a quiet habitation,
> A tabernacle that will not be taken down;
> Not one of its stakes will ever be removed,
> Nor will any of its cords be broken.
>
> But there the majestic Lord will be for us
> A place of broad rivers and streams,
> In which no galley with oars will sail,
> Nor majestic ships pass by
>
> (For the Lord is our Judge,
> The Lord is our Lawgiver,
> The Lord is our King;
> He will save us);
>
> Your tackle is loosed,

> They could not strengthen their mast,
> They could not spread the sail.

I will be the first to recognize that this passage, in its historical context, has little to do with strategic-level spiritual warfare or taking a city for God. Nevertheless, we felt it was God's prophetic word for The Dwelling Place Church in Hemet, California, in 1991, so we set out to obey it and apply it as we sensed God's leading step-by-step.

Isaiah speaks of a tabernacle held down by a stake driven into the ground. The stake would never be removed. A stake in Hemet? As I continued in prayer, I sensed that the Lord was telling us to drive stakes into the ground. I had never heard of anyone else doing this, nor would I be surprised if no one else ever did it. But I knew in my spirit it would be right for us, particularly if the elders of the church agreed.

I called the elders together early one Sunday morning, explaining to them that I sensed the Lord was telling us to drive stakes into the ground in order to secure the spiritual canopy He wanted to spread over the city. We prayed together and as we did we felt of one mind in the Lord. We agreed to move out and take action in a way that might seem strange not only to our neighbors, but also to us. We decided to do it that very afternoon. One of the elders who had a woodworking shop volunteered to make the two-by-two oak stakes for us.

That morning in both services I shared with the congregation that we were going on another intercessory excursion, or what Kjell Sjöberg refers to in chapter 4 as a prophetic prayer action. "Come dressed casual and meet at the church at 4:30 P.M." I announced. We would break up into five groups. Four groups would accompany an elder with a stake to one of the four main entrances into our valley—all being highways. The fifth group would accompany my wife and me to the main intersection in the middle of town. At precisely 5:00 P.M., each elder would drive his stake into the ground as a memorial unto the Lord, and the resulting canopy of prayer would remain as our declaration of strategic intercessory warfare against the encroaching darkness.

At the same time, Susan and I, standing by the intersection in the center of town, would simultaneously lift up a praise offering unto the Lord as a center pole of the spiritual canopy. We would then return to the church for the normal 6:00 P.M. service at which time we would share our experience together with the whole group.

When directing each elder where to drive their respective stakes, I selected each location by my map. I asked the elder and the group that went to the northern side of the valley to drive their stake adjacent to Massacre Canyon and the Church of Scientology. On each stake was inscribed the Scripture from Isaiah 33:20-24.

Broad Rivers, Streams and Ships

Upon our return, the elder of the group that returned from the northern entrance had made a remarkable discovery. As they were reading the inscribed Scriptures out loud, they realized that Isaiah 33:21 spoke of the Lord being a place of "broad rivers and streams." One of the men noticed that immediately in front of them was the now dry San Jacinto riverbed and to their immediate left sat the now dry Massacre Canyon streambed. Both are now dry due to the water line disaster and the exploitation of the water company mentioned previously.

This would have been encouragement enough, but there was more. The passage specifically mentions ships with tackle, mast and sails. We live in a desert community, far from nautical objects. Nevertheless, the elder explained to the congregation that night that after they had driven the stake and on their way back to church, they passed by the headquarters of the Church of Scientology and to their amazement saw, on the Scientology grounds and up against the foothills, a huge full-scale replica of a three-masted schooner complete with tackle, masts and sails!

We all broke out into a shout of praise to God at the realization of the incredible odds of finding all three of these together: the riverbed, the streambed, and a ship with tackle, mast and sails in the middle of the desert. Needless to say, we were greatly encouraged to press on in intercession for the deliverance of our community. We believed that the Lord Himself had graciously given us tangible signs that He was leading and directing our activities.

After this spiritual canopy was raised up, the flow of information regarding activity of darkness in our community dramatically increased. People seemed to come out of nowhere with information about old buildings, past misuse of land or a "friend of a friend" who knew of a witch holding meetings somewhere. We began to see immediate results from our new, accurate intercession through spiritual mapping.

New Life for the Church
The results of our strategic-level intercession and our prophetic prayer actions proved to have a dramatic effect on the life of our own congregation. In the past, if we were known for anything, we were known for church splits. We had experienced 5 splits in 18 years. Disunity is now a thing of the past. The warm spirit of love and harmony is drawing in new people and our church has been growing as never before.

For 15 years we had met in an old, partially refurbished drive-up dairy where my office was the creamery and separator room, and the nursery was the old freezer box. The upgrades had been few. We had struggled through many fundraising programs in an effort to raise the much-needed finances to do the necessary remodeling just to meet the basic needs of the congregation.

Our congregational members were mostly blue-collar workers and our financial ability never seemed to be quite enough to get us under way. The congregation, as well as the leadership, felt helpless to change matters.

But something was now happening and it was truly the unmistakable hand of God. After entering into this level of intercession, our own congregation raised enough money in a period of only 18 months to build an entirely new children's facility (debt free). In that same period of time we completely remodeled the sanctuary (the old dairy). And the congregation doubled in size in less than a year's time!

New Hope for the Community

The result of this type of intercession and dealing with strongholds of darkness has openly changed the spiritual face of our community. As many as 35 ministers in our city now work together for evangelism. They meet monthly for a time of prayer and support for one another. Churches share their resources such as copy machines, projectors and other office equipment. One church shares its children's ministries building each week with another church that is without a permanent meeting place. It is no longer uncommon to hear of pastors swapping pulpits with one another on Sunday mornings. One pastor invited the pastor of another church in our city to come to his church, dedicate his newly born daughter to the Lord before his congregation, and then stay to preach the morning service.

Recently 30 churches and ministries of the city came together for a 2-week tent revival. Every night of the revival a different pastor from the community preached and a different church provided the music. Each night, for 2 solid weeks, the tent was filled to capacity with members from congregations throughout our valley bringing their unsaved friends to hear the gospel. Many were saved, healed and delivered in this open show of unity by the corporate Body of Christ in our valley.

I have read in Jeremiah 9:3 how God's people at one time

were not "valiant for the truth on the earth." We used to fit this description, but we are changing. I believe we will take our cities, one at a time, by becoming not only a "name and a praise and a glory" unto the Lord, but by stepping out from behind the confines of our church buildings, church activities, church programs and church traditions, and literally becoming a people for the Lord who are valiant for the truth upon the earth!

■ REFLECTION QUESTIONS ■

1. Bob Beckett expresses his frustration because, although prayers for individual people were being answered, prayers for the community seemed ineffectual. Can you identify with this? What can be done about it?

2. Analyze the prayer meeting in the mountain cabin dealing with a "bearhide" in light of what we learned in Kjell Sjöberg's chapter on "prophetic prayer actions."

3. Jesus addressed cities as personalities. Do you think you could do this? Could it be done in corporate prayer meetings in your church?

4. How important do you think it is for a pastor to make a "territorial commitment"? Do you know any pastors who have made territorial commitments? Would they agree with Beckett?

5. Does Bob Beckett think that all of us ought to go out and drive stakes with Bible verses on them in the ground? Does it sound like something you and your friends would do?

Notes

1. John Dawson, *Taking Our Cities for God* (Lake Mary, FL: Creation House, 1989).
2. Cindy Jacobs, *Possessing the Gates of the Enemy* (Tarrytown, NY: Chosen Books, 1991).

Evangelizing a City Dedicated to Darkness

by Victor Lorenzo

VICTOR LORENZO WORKS IN HIS NATIVE LAND OF ARGENTINA with Harvest Evangelism. His gifts of discernment have equipped him for extensive spiritual mapping in the cities of Resistencia and La Plata. He was ordained to the ministry in the Vision of the Future Church under the Reverend Omar Cabrera. Victor serves as the Southern Cone Area Secretary for the Spiritual Warfare Network of the A.D. 2000 United Prayer Track.

Whenever we address the subject of spiritual warfare in general and spiritual mapping in particular, I believe it is helpful to clarify the role of the Church in this activity.

THE CHURCH'S MANDATE

The Church has a mandate to preach the gospel throughout the world and to advance the Kingdom of God and His righteousness. Spiritual warfare and spiritual mapping are simply activities that aid the fulfillment of this mandate. They help us discover and destroy the strategies and wiles Satan has used to keep people under his dominion, blinded to the glorious message of Jesus Christ.

As accurate as spiritual mapping might be, it is my opinion that without an explicit focus on evangelization, it has little meaning. It is not an end in itself. Likewise, evangelism that does not take seriously our engagement with demonic powers through spiritual warfare can turn out to be an effort with minimal results.

God has given authority to His Church and its leaders to take neighborhoods, cities, nations as well as continents for Jesus Christ. The effectiveness of the Church in winning unbelievers to Christ and in improving society will depend greatly on its readiness to undertake this battle. Spiritual unity among the churches and dedication to intercessory prayer are important prerequisites for victory.

GOD'S CALL TO SPIRITUAL MAPPING

My call to spiritual mapping came through my involvement in "Plan Resistencia," a massive evangelistic effort focused on the city of Resistencia, Argentina. I am currently involved in the ministry of Harvest Evangelism under the leadership of Edgardo Silvoso, a fellow Argentine. We had agreed as a team to launch a 3-year evangelistic outreach in Resistencia, a city of 400,000 in northern Argentina. Our major emphases were to be the unity of the Body of Christ in Resistencia, to undertake strategic-level spiritual warfare, to conduct intensive intercessory prayer, to multiply new churches, along with employing the traditional methods of evangelism. During the first year, the Holy Spirit began to show us that the magnitude of the required spiritual warfare was much greater than we had imagined.

My own vision for spiritual warfare was greatly enlarged in early 1990. I began to see that spiritual warfare was to be done on the ground level—casting out demons that tormented people—as well as on the strategic level. This was a dimension of demonic strategy that turned out to be both complex and widespread. When I read John Dawson's book, *Taking Our Cities for God* (Creation House), I began to think about the need for applying Dawson's principles to Resistencia. But I was reluctant. I had ministered to many people who were in bondage to evil spirits and knew firsthand the horrors of the devil's activities. I did not have any inclination to go more deeply into the secrets of satanic strategy.

Gonzalo and the Guardian Angel

My reluctance to do what by then I knew to be God's will provided an opening for the enemy to attack both me and my family. Every night for a whole week our 15-month-old son, Gonzalo, would awaken at 1:00 A.M. screaming. Each night it required up to four hours to calm him down. Finally, one night I felt I had had enough and I needed to take a different form of action. I knew that my rebellious attitude was at the root of our problem. I asked my wife to stay in bed while I dealt with it.

Before going to Gonzalo's bedroom I went to the dining room to pray. I said, "Lord please forgive me for my disobedience. I confess that I have no resources or ability in myself to handle this situation. I pray that you will open my eyes and my ears to understand what your Holy Spirit desires to reveal to me. God, please give me the same anointing that Elisha had to perceive spiritual reality. Permit me to see my enemies, but also give me the confidence that those who are with me are more numerous and more powerful than those against me. May I see the reality of your angels."

Having faith that the Lord would respond to my prayer, I went into little Gonzalo's bedroom. When I opened the door, I was overwhelmed with an awesome force of evil. I felt cold chills. Immediately I sensed the presence of death, and knew the Lord was revealing the identity of my enemy.

I sensed the Holy Spirit saying to me, "Take authority in the name of Jesus," and I obeyed. I commanded the spirit of death to get out and never return to torment my son. At that moment, I saw in my mind a painting of a guardian angel with which I was familiar.

I said, "Lord, You have promised that You would put angels around us for our protection. If it is Your will, I need that protection now, especially for my family." Immediately the bedroom was filled with a brilliant light. I looked toward the crib where Gonzalo was lying and I saw a huge angel holding a drawn sword. The angel said to me, "From this day on I will be at your son's side to protect him and care for him while you fulfill your divine calling."

Gonzalo is now three years old and has never again been tormented by evil spirits. The little boy has an unusual understanding of spiritual warfare and he himself now takes authority in the name of Jesus over any power of darkness that he is able to perceive.

Mapping Resistencia

I now knew that God wanted me to research the city of Resistencia. I was also painfully aware that I had no training or experience in such things. My only tool was John Dawson's *Taking Our Cities for God.*[1] I took Dawson's questions and went to the city library. After four days of plowing through hundreds of pages, I was totally frustrated. I had to admit that although I now had a great deal of accurate information, I had not discovered a thing that seemed important to our task.

Humbled by this experience, I went once again to prayer. I begged the Holy Spirit to give me new revelation and show me the way ahead. When I arrived home, my wife, not knowing many details about what I was doing, suggested I visit a local exposition of native art. Without fully understanding why, I had a feeling that if I followed her suggestion I would find some answers.

Sure enough. When I went to the exposition, I met 5 university professors who were more than willing to share information with me. They agreed that it was important to understand the spiritual identity of Resistencia. They gave me information that was totally new to me. For 10 days and in an absolutely incredible manner, these 5 scholars provided all I needed. I was amazed at the powerful hand of God in all of this. It was hard to believe that these 5 men, well-known and respected throughout the city, were actually working for me!

The Powers over the City

From the information I received through the city's folklore, I was able to identify four spiritual powers: *San La Muerte* (spirit of death), *Pombero* (spirit of fear), *Curupí* (spirit of sexual perversion) and *Pitón* (Python or the spirit of witchcraft and sorcery).

Having this data, and not knowing exactly what to do with it, I asked the Lord once again to show me the way. His answer this time was, "Wait." I waited for a month and a half, then Cindy Jacobs visited Argentina for the first time. Harvest Evangelism was sending her to help instruct Christian leaders and intercessors in spiritual warfare.

Accompanied by Doris Wagner, Cindy ministered in Buenos Aires with remarkable power and then arrived in Resistencia for a two-day seminar. On the first day I shared with her the information I had gathered. I told her of four large modern art murals in the central plaza, which I thought might present for us a spiritual map of the city.

When Cindy saw the panels that afternoon, the Lord, through her gift of discernment of spirits, clearly showed her

---

Spiritual mapping combines research, divine revelation, and confirmatory evidence in order to provide complete and exact data concerning the identity, strategies and methods employed by spiritual forces of darkness to influence the people and the churches of a given region.

---

the invisible behind the visible, as Peter Wagner discusses in chapter 2. She confirmed the presence of the four principalities over Resistencia, then she discerned two others. These were high ranking principalities she had first encountered in Buenos Aires and whom she suspected might have national jurisdiction—the spirit of Freemasonry and *Reina del Cielo*, the Queen of Heaven.

During the seminar, Cindy, who was skillfully interpreted by Marfa Cabrera, shared deep and revealing insights. She led us to a much broader understanding of spiritual warfare, as well as coaching the church leaders in practical ways of taking the land in Jesus' name.

The Battle in the Plaza
The next day our team went out to the plaza with the pastors of the Resistencia churches, a group of trained intercessors and

Cindy Jacobs. We battled fiercely against the invisible powers over the city for four hours. We attacked them in what we sensed was their hierarchical order, from bottom to top. First came *Pombero*, then *Curupí*, then *San La Muerte*, then spirit of Freemasonry, then Queen of Heaven, then the Python spirit whom we suspected functioned as the coordinator of all the forces of evil in the city. When we finished, an almost tangible sense of peace and freedom came over all who had participated. We were confident that this first battle had been won and that the city could be claimed for the Lord.

After this, the church in Resistencia was ready for full-scale evangelization. Unbelievers began to respond to the gospel as never before. As a result of our three-year outreach, church attendance increased by 102 percent. The effect was felt in all social strata of the city. We could undertake community projects such as providing drinking water for the poor. The public image of the evangelical church improved greatly by gaining respect and approval from political and social leaders. We were invited to use the media to spread our message. The spiritual warfare and mapping we were able to do opened new doors in Resistencia for evangelism, social improvement and reaping of the spiritual harvest.

WHAT IS SPIRITUAL MAPPING?

As I see it, spiritual mapping combines research, divine revelation, and confirmatory evidence in order to provide complete and exact data concerning the identity, strategies and methods employed by spiritual forces of darkness to influence the people and the churches of a given region.

Is This Biblical?

Although the Bible does not use our contemporary term "spiritual mapping," we see it is one of many procedural activities in the process of conducting biblical spiritual warfare. It is biblical to be aware of the "wiles of the devil" (see 2 Cor. 2:11, *AMP),* and spiritual mapping simply helps us to do that. To me it is like saying that citywide crusades are biblical because they are

---

Spiritual mapping is like the intelligence forces of an army. Through it, we go behind enemy lines to understand the enemy's plans and fortifications. We do..."spiritual espionage."

---

a means to biblical evangelism or that Sunday Schools are biblical as a means to biblical Christian nurture even though neither is mentioned in the Bible.

Spiritual mapping is like the intelligence forces of an army. Through it, we go behind enemy lines to understand the enemy's plans and fortifications. As Kjell Sjöberg says in chapter 4, we do "spiritual espionage."

In the Old Testament, we see a model for taking cities through the experience of Israel. The Israelites sent spies first to size up the enemy. In Numbers 13, for example, we find the Israelites in position to enter the Promised Land. Moses sent 12 spies. They went with the authority of Moses and of God. They had clear instructions on what they were to investigate. They returned with the information, along with a negative majority opinion. The result? Forty years in the wilderness!

Then in Joshua 2 the Israelites had another chance to enter the Promised Land. Joshua sent out two spies. They had authority. They received clear instructions. They collected the information from a member of the enemy's camp, Rahab. They brought back the information *without* a personal opinion. The result? The conquest of Jericho!

In Joshua 7, the Israelites were to conquer Ai. They sent spies, but there was sin in their camp. They had "holes in their armor" as Cindy Jacobs would say. They were sent at the wrong time, they were deceived, and they gave a defective report. The result? The Israelites were defeated!

From these and other passages, I draw several principles for spiritual mapping, which I believe are biblical principles:

1. We must base our ministry on God's Word and His revelation.

2. We must be certain we are living in holiness before we go forth.

3. We must be sent by God in His time and with His authority.

4. We must conduct our research according to the instructions we have received.

5. We must report our information without personal or prejudicial opinions.

6. We must keep an attitude of faith in the power of God.

A NEW CHALLENGE: LA PLATA

Partly as a result of the ministry in Resistencia, the ministerial association of the city of La Plata invited Harvest Evangelism to conduct a new three-year outreach project in partnership with them. We hoped that lessons learned in Resistencia would help us to do an even better job in La Plata.

For us, Resistencia was an experimental laboratory where, under unusually stressful conditions, we could field-test each aspect of our plan. Our laboratory turned up both strengths and weaknesses. One thing we had learned was that the success of any such plan would depend on the attitude of the pastors of the city and the readiness of the churches for such a project. We concluded that the lack of penetration of a city using effective evangelization has a direct relationship to the spiritual condition of the churches.

In La Plata, we wanted to repeat what we did right in Resistencia and avoid what we did wrong. We believe that the permanent results of any citywide evangelistic effort will be in direct proportion to the success of the spiritual battles in which the ruling forces of the city are engaged. At the same time, the final victory will depend on the internal spiritual health of the churches. For the churches to be healthy, the pastors and other leaders need to honestly face any sinful conditions that give place to the devil. They must learn to use the spiritual weapons the Lord has given to His church. They must reject any form or appearance of rebellion, strife and division.

After three intense years of work in Resistencia, we saw many signs and wonders, we saw a city open to the preaching of the gospel of Christ, we saw social improvement, and we gained favor in the eyes of the unbelievers. On the other hand, we did not succeed in healing the wounds of bitterness among all pastors. Therefore, although the unity of the churches had improved considerably, it did not fully meet the desires of the heart of God. Some leaders did not have the courage to come openly against the strongholds the enemy had planted among the churches. As a result, the churches were more vulnerable to spiritual attacks than they needed to be and the project was not as successful as we would have hoped.

By way of footnote, we are thankful that at this writing the situation has improved greatly, and the Body of Christ in Resistencia is finally coming together in spiritual unity. If this had happened two or three years ago, we feel we would have seen much more fruit that remains than we did. Nevertheless, an increase in church attendance of 102 percent is heartening.

Moving into La Plata

The evangelistic plan for La Plata continues the vision that God has given to Edgardo Silvoso for strategizing city taking for Christ. Silvoso bases his strategy on four fundamental principles:

1. The spiritual unity of the churches of a city;
2. Powerful intercessory prayer;
3. Strategic-level spiritual warfare;
4. Multiplication of new churches.

Peter Wagner says, "The most sophisticated strategy for evangelizing a city we have at the present time is Edgardo Silvoso's Harvest Evangelism."[2] To see how spiritual mapping fits into the whole evangelistic design, allow me to summarize Ed Silvoso's six steps for taking a city:

1. Establish God's perimeter in the city.

Define who and how many make up the Kingdom of God in the city. Search out the "faithful remnant," those who have made a commitment to pay the price that revival might come.

2. Strengthen the perimeter.

Recognize that the enemy has infiltrated the city as well as the churches. Nurture and edify the saints. Discern the enemy's strongholds. "Keep the unity of the Spirit in the bond of peace" (Eph. 4:3). Initiate the prayer movement and establish prayer houses in the city.

3. Expand God's perimeter in the city.

Make specific plans to extend the Kingdom of God in the city. Formulate goals and objectives. Take advantage of every resource available. Begin to train leaders and church planters.

4. Infiltrate Satan's perimeter.

Launch the "air attack" of specific and strategic intercessory prayer through hundreds or thousands of prayer houses (prayer cells), having the objective of weakening Satan's control over the unsaved, claiming instead a favorable disposition to the gospel. At the same time begin to plant embryonic churches ("lighthouses") in anticipation of an abundant harvest.

5. Attack and destroy Satan's perimeter.

Begin the "frontal assault." Launch the spiritual takeover of the city, confronting, binding and casting down the spiritual powers ruling over the region. Proclaim the message of the gospel to every person in the city. Disciple the new believers through the established "lighthouses."

6. Establish God's new perimeter
where Satan's once existed.

Baptize new believers in a united baptismal service as a visible and spiritual declaration of victory. Continue discipling. Build up the new churches. Inject the missionary vision to reach other cities. Repeat the cycle!

As I write, the La Plata plan has not yet reached its midpoint. It began in 1991, having a goal to see 5 percent of the population become evangelical Christians by the end of 1993. This will mean that the 85 Christian churches existing in 1991 will need to be increased to 300 churches by the end of 1993. As of now, 1,700 prayer houses have been started and many intensive training seminars have been held. In June 1992, Cindy Jacobs visited La Plata for the second time. On Cindy's first visit, she conducted a seminar on inner healing for the church members who, in general, were not in excellent spiritual health. On Cindy's second visit, as I will detail later, she led the pastors and intercessors in beginning to take spiritual authority over the city, intensifying the "air attack."

THE SPIRITUAL MAPPING BEGINS

In Edgardo Silvoso's evangelistic design, the spiritual mapping should be largely done before step number 5, "Attack and destroy Satan's perimeter." Under my direction, most of the spiritual mapping had been done before Cindy Jacob's visit in June.

A short time before my family and I moved from Resistencia to La Plata, I went aside for a time of prayer. I asked the Lord to show me the spiritual situation in La Plata. I sensed the Lord speaking to me and, somewhat to my surprise, giving me only one word: "Freemasonry." I immediately recalled that one of the ruling spirits over Resistencia, and one that Cindy Jacobs and Doris Wagner had suspected was a national territorial spirit, was the spirit of Freemasonry. I knew something of the role Freemasonry played in the liberation of Latin America from the Spaniards through Simón Bolivar and José de San Martín. But other than that, I had no personal knowledge at all about the secret order, what it believed or what it did.

When I arrived in La Plata, I first sought out and established relationships with the recognized intercessors from several churches. Having no communication between themselves and without my mentioning a thing about it, three intercessors volunteered the information that in prayer they had recently been warned against the spirit of Freemasonry. This confirmed the message I had received from the Lord and gave me confidence to move along that track in my research.

The Founders of La Plata

My research confirmed that all of those who participated in the founding of the city a little more than one hundred years ago were Masons. Dardo Rocha, known as the father of the city, was a high-ranking Mason. The founders belonged to the Masonic Lodge of Eastern Argentina. The book published by the newspaper *El Día* to commemorate the one hundredth anniversary of the founding of La Plata, says, "The city of La Plata was created to give refuge to the Masonic family of Eastern Argentina."

A City Planned to Glorify the Enemy

On the next page I am reproducing a map of the 1,254 city blocks of the central part of La Plata to illustrate what appears to be the intentional design of the founders of the city to glorify the creature rather than the Creator. The key number is 6, prominent in the occult, plazas being spaced every 6 blocks. The number 666 is clearly displayed on many of the public buildings. The point of highest altitude in the city is the central plaza from which the 2 major diagonal boulevards, Diagonals 73 and 74, descend to the 4 cardinal points of the compass. The city is not laid out north, south, east and west, as are most Latin American cities, but at a 45-degree angle so that the diagonals, not the ordinary streets, line up with the points of the compass. As can be seen, the diagonals form an almost perfect pyramid.

In the process of establishing the new city of La Plata, Dardo Rocha visited Egypt, the land of the pyramids and also the ancient homeland of Freemasonry. There he purchased 16 mummies, presumably with the intention of helping to secure the city permanently under the power of dark angels. Today 4 of them are housed in the Natural Science Museum. No one I have contacted knows where the other 12 are, but some historians suspect that they lie buried in strategic points of the city where their potential occult power could influence the greatest number of inhabitants.

The Four Women

In the central plaza, Plaza Moreno, are four large statues at first appearing as attractive women. Closer examination shows that each of the women has made the sign of the curse by extending the index and little fingers of one hand. One of them, on Diagonal 73 toward the west, is pointing at the Catholic Cathe-

Map of La Plata

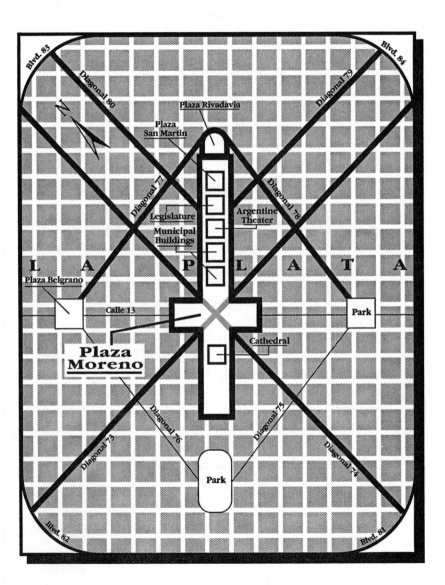

dral, cursing the religious power over the city. A second statue, on the eastern part of Diagonal 73, is holding wheat that has been deformed in one hand, and her other hand is cursing the ground, the source of our daily bread. The third statue is on the north side of Diagonal 74. She is in a sensual posture offering a flower with one hand and in the other holding a bouquet of flowers along with the sign of the curse. She is cursing everything that is involved in love and the family. The fourth statue is on the south of Diagonal 74, extending her hand toward City Hall and cursing the political power of the city.

When I began to investigate the origin of these wicked statues, I found that they had been selected and ordered from a catalog issued by the Val D'Osme Foundry in Paris, France, a foundry owned and operated by Freemasons. I also discovered, much to my chagrin, that most of the statues in plazas all over Argentina were manufactured by the same Masonic foundry.

Also in the central plaza, and from the same foundry, are two large urns in the Masonic tradition whose handles are shaped like demonic faces.

After gathering all this information about the role of Freemasonry in the founding of La Plata, I still did not feel I had as yet discovered the real key to the spiritual mapping. I went to prayer for several days, asking the Lord to show me more. One day I sensed I was hearing Him say, "The key you are seeking is drawn on the map of the city."

LA PLATA: A MASONIC TEMPLE?

If we look at the map of La Plata more closely, we begin to see that the overall geometric design forms basic Masonic symbolism.

1. The compass. The hinge of the Masonic compass is formed by the Plaza Rivadavia, named after the first president of Argentina who was a Freemason, and the Plaza Almirante Brown, named after a military officer who participated in the revolution against Spain and who also was a Freemason. The two arms of the compass come down on Diagonals 77 and 78.

2. Square. The inside of the Masonic square forms a right angle point at Plaza San Martín, named for Argentina's national hero who was a Freemason. The outside forms a right angle point at Plaza Moreno, where the four notorious statues are also located. Moreno was a key figure in the May 1810 Revolution and a Freemason.

3. Inverted cross. As can be seen on the map, the inverted cross is formed by what is called "The Historic Axis of the City," containing the buildings housing the religious and political powers of La Plata. The vertical point of the cross begins with the police station at the foot of the cross (the top part of the map, because it is inverted), runs through the Provincial Government headquarters, the Provincial Legislature, the Argentine theater, the city hall, the Catholic cathedral, the Ministry of Health and ends with the army headquarters. To the left of the crossbar is the courthouse and to the right the Ministry of Education.

A principle of democratic government is to keep the branches independent of each other. But I have found that many cities designed by Masons feature underground secret tunnels to link them. In La Plata, 52nd Street, also called The Historic Axis of the City, has no surface street, but has a tunnel underneath. Some say that the Masons conducted secret rituals under the centers of power in the city, thus exercising, to the extent possible, spiritual control over the people.

Because Masons do not believe that Jesus' blood shed on the Cross is the only payment for our sins and thus the only way to salvation, it appears from the map that the X formed by the major Diagonals 73 and 74 visually crosses out or cancels the Cross. They cross at the cornerstone of the city in the center of Plaza Moreno, which is said to contain a Masonic time capsule implanted by Dardo Rocha.

Although I have not highlighted them on the map, I have found further Masonic symbols in the design of the city streets such as the Eastern Star, the pentagram and others. Additional symbols are present in the form of statues and monuments throughout the city.

After doing some additional research in the United States in early 1992, I am now prepared to offer the hypothesis that La Plata could well be the epitome of Masonic city designs. I would also not be surprised if the city itself is regarded as a central temple for Freemasonry on the entire American continent.

What Is Freemasonry?

My studies have indicated that Freemasonry is a secret occultic movement, worshiping and serving Satan and the demonic powers. It uses whatever means are available to gain power, authority and influence in human affairs. It is a combination of many beliefs, having roots in ancient Egypt and moving through Assyria, Chaldea, Babylonia, China, India, Scandinavia, Rome and Greece.

Many join the Masons because they perceive it as a fraternal and benevolent association. While rising through the orders, demonization is likely to occur, and at the top degrees, overt and irreversible pacts are reportedly made with Satan and his forces. The ultimate outcome in many cases may not be benevolence, but an aid to Satan's objectives to steal, kill and destroy.

A modern outcome of Freemasonry relates to the growing New Age movement. In fact, *The New Age Magazine* is published by "The Mother Supreme Council of the World, The Supreme Council of the Thirty-Third and Last Degree, Ancient and Accepted Scottish Rite of Freemasonry, Southern Jurisdiction, U.S.A.," headquartered in Washington, DC.

The Powers over La Plata

Through our study of Freemasonry and its beliefs, we feel we have discovered the presence of six spiritual principalities that rule in La Plata. These territorial spirits are:

1. Spirit of sensuality: exhibited in the common phallic symbolism of Freemasonry.

2. Spirit of violence: rooted in methods of punishment built into Masonic initiation rites.

3. Spirit of witchcraft: manifested in the magic and intrigue of Freemasonry.

4. Spirit of living death: related to the legend of the Egyptian Osiris, and perpetuated in La Plata through the rituals of burying the mummies to curse the city.

5. The Masonic deity, Jah-Bal-On: who is the strongman over the city.

6. The Queen of Heaven: manifested primarily in the worship of the Virgin Mary, and possibly related through Freemasonry to the ancient Egyptian goddess Isis.

Many lines through the city undoubtedly constitute occultic power lines. The Historic Axis of the City where 52nd Street should be is a prime example. Another is Diagonal 74, which goes through the Central Plaza where the four statues are located, through many other important plazas, through the location of a colony of Afro-Brazilians who openly practice voodoo and curses of death, and ending in the cemetery, a symbol of death.

TAKING AUTHORITY OVER LA PLATA

A year of spiritual mapping and many other preparatory activities took place, including a citywide inner healing seminar, the creation of a powerful network of intercessors, many pastors' prayer gatherings, and the establishment of 1,700 prayer houses. By June 1992, the pastors of the city felt it was time for the first spiritual battle against the predominant satanic forces of La Plata. Cindy Jacobs, who is well respected among Argentine leaders for her spiritual gifts and ministry in directing pastors to take their city for God, visited La Plata to participate.

The pastors took as their directional text 2 Chronicles 7:14: "If My people who are called by My name will humble themselves, and pray and seek My face, and turn from their wicked ways, then I will hear from heaven, and will forgive their sin and heal their land."

The believers of the city gathered in one of the principal churches. For four hours, the church of La Plata fervently prayed for the city, asking forgiveness for the iniquities of the community and the sins being committed. The leaders humbly begged God to erase the consequences of the sin and to remove the curse from the city. They prayed for those who had been wounded by the political leaders and the unjust social structures, and for those wounded by the churches and by church leaders. They repented for the presence of Freemasonry in the city and for delivering the city to Satan. They poured out their hearts asking forgiveness for all manner of sexual sins, for violence in the city (especially during the terrorist era), for military oppression, for worship of the principality known as the Queen of Heaven, and for witchcraft and sorcery in the city. Finally they came against the spirit of living death and the resulting apathy among the people.

After an extended time of humility and repentance shedding many tears, they were ready to proclaim: "Now is God's time for La Plata!"

After that remarkable event, and feeling that God had answered our prayers for deliverance and forgiveness of sins, 20 pastors and several intercessors met with Cindy Jacobs and her husband, Mike, to plan a strategy to do battle in the central plaza, the Plaza Moreno. The rest of the group stayed behind, praying for our protection. It was decided that the pastors at the Plaza Moreno would pray two by two, the first pastor breaking the power of the spirit and the second calling forth the opposite spirit and God's redemptive gift using Scriptures. One at a time they prayed:

1. Against the spirit of sensuality: They would pray standing on the cornerstone of the city on Diagonal 73, facing east toward Europe from which came the first settlers of the area, who were mostly criminals and prostitutes.

2. Against the spirit of violence: We would pray on Diagonal 73 facing west and looking into the interior of the nation where cruel attacks were launched against the Indian population, causing much bloodshed and the annihilation of some of the tribes.

3. Against the spirit of witchcraft: on Diagonal 74 facing north toward Brazil from which came the Afro-Brazilian spiritism.

4. Against the spirit of living death: on Diagonal 74 facing south in the direction of the cemetery, symbol of death.

5. Against the spirit of the Queen of Heaven: facing the Cathedral, which represented the cult of worship of the Virgin Mary.

6. Against the Masonic deity, Jah-Bal-On: the strongman over the city standing on the city cornerstone.

We began to pray at 6:00 P.M., believing that the number 6 was important, and we prayed in the above order. We felt that God gave us some significant signs during our time there. For example, when we began praying against the spirit of violence and destruction, the bells in city hall rang for no apparent reason. We had seen the identical thing happen both in Mar del Plata and Resistencia, thus we interpreted it as a divine sign. We later discovered that back at the church at the exact moment we were binding the spirit of violence, demons manifested in a young man who had been involved in the martial arts. He jumped nine feet in the air, bashed his head against a wall and began smashing tables and chairs. The believers prayed deliverance over him and he was freed from the satanic attack.

Later, as we stood on the cornerstone of the city in the center of Plaza Moreno, we came against the spirit of Freemasonry and felt freedom in the Holy Spirit to break the curses over the diagonal ley lines of the city. We proclaimed that there would be a new city having Jesus Christ as the cornerstone of La Plata. We then formed ourselves in the shape of a cross in the center of the plaza on the city cornerstone, lifting Jesus high over the city and restoring the cross, right side up, as a symbol of salvation for the city of La Plata.

CONCLUSION

We still have many months remaining in our evangelistic outreach for La Plata. We believe the results will be even greater than in Resistencia. As I conclude this chapter, we are in the midst of a citywide evangelistic crusade with Carlos Annacondia, one of God's most powerful evangelists. Significantly, the crusade is being held at the army headquarters exactly at the foot of the inverted cross (which would be the top of the upright cross). I rejoice in what is happening and what will happen, and for the privilege of making a small contribution to the extension of the Kingdom of God through spiritual mapping.

■ REFLECTION QUESTIONS ■

1. Some will find it hard to believe that Victor Lorenzo actually saw an angel. Do you think it is possible? Do you know anyone personally who has seen an angel?
2. Review Lorenzo's six principles for spiritual mapping on page 179. Give a reason of your own for each principle.
3. Edgardo Silvoso's strategy for citywide evangelism incorporates strategic-level spiritual warfare and spiritual mapping. Do you know of any other citywide strategy that does this?
4. Study the map of La Plata. Be sure you can pinpoint the features described by Lorenzo. Why would someone want to design a city on occultic patterns?
5. What influence does Freemasonry have in your community? How is it perceived by the general public? By the Christian community?

Notes
1. John Dawson, *Taking Our Cities for God* (Lake Mary, FL: Creation House, 1989), p. 85.
2. C. Peter Wagner, *Warfare Prayer* (Ventura, CA: Regal Books, 1992), p. 162.

Part III: Application

RONGHOLDS...

Mapping and Discerning Seattle, Washington

ᵍ H T

by Mark McGregor and Bev Klopp

MARK MCGREGOR IS A COMPUTER PROGRAMMER LIVING IN
Seattle, Washington, and taking courses in the
Fuller Theological Seminary extension center in
Seattle.

*Bev Klopp is founder of Gateway Ministries, which helps
churches strategize prayer, spiritual warfare and evangelism for their cities. A recognized intercessor, Bev is a
member of the intercession team serving the Spiritual
Warfare Network and the United Prayer Track of the
A.D. 2000 and Beyond Movement.*

SECTION I: MAPPING SEATTLE, MARK McGREGOR

This document is based upon the 20 questions on page 85 in John Dawson's book *Taking Our Cities for God.*[1] The purpose of these 20 questions, according to Dawson, is to examine the history of a city or country to help determine two things: (1) areas of past sin that need repentance and forgiveness; and (2) the redemptive gifts of the city. Why is this important?

First, Dawson holds that the past sins of a city or nation can open the area to demonic spiritual influences and powers, which can gain control over the city and keep it and the people in spiritual bondage.

Second, Dawson holds that God has granted certain redemptive "gifts" to each city, and that the enemy seeks to pervert these gifts so that the city bears no spiritual fruit. Dawson believes that the Christian leaders need to discover both the past sins and the redemptive gifts of their city in order to break the powers that bind the city and move into the true spiritual environment God intended.

1. What place does your city have in this nation's history?

The Washington territory came into being when England and America finally decided to settle the issue of national boundaries. America claimed, and received, everything between the 48th parallel and the Columbia River, with the exception of Victoria Island. The first settlers arrived in the Seattle area in the early 1850s, migrating up from the Oregon territory. The initial industries were fur and timber, the otter furs going to China and the timber to San Francisco, which was booming due to the gold rush.

The city of Seattle began to grow following the Civil War. It played no part in the war, although by stance and law it was not a slavery territory. Growth occurred in spurts, as there was no strong stable industry for the region. The Fraser, and later the Yukon, gold strikes helped Seattle grow, as it was a natural stopping off point for coastal travel. It became, and still is, the major transit point between Alaska and the lower 48 states.

Seattle developed as an industrial city and a trade center, centered on shipping with both Alaska and the Far East. Ship

---

It is important to examine the history of a city or country to help determine (1) areas of past sin that need repentance and forgiveness and, (2) the redemptive gifts of the city or country.

---

and airplane building were two major industries. During World War II, Seattle was a central city in the war effort because of its strategic location on the Pacific, and because of the impact of the Boeing Corporation. This time period was probably the most significant for Seattle in modern history.

2. Was there ever the imposition of a new culture or language through conquest?

Yes, although conquest might not be the best term to describe the events.

When whites first came to the region, the Indian tribes belonged to the "Coast Salish" language group, and had a distinct hunter/gatherer culture centered around salmon fishing. Along with whites came the influence of Spanish, French, English, Russian and American cultures. An intermediate language, "Chinook," evolved, which was a combination of Salish, French, and English. Many Indians, including Chief Seattle, resented this language, but whites essentially refused to learn

Salish, and would generally only communicate in English or possibly Chinook.

The coming of the white culture also spelled the beginning of the end of Indian culture, as well as the decimation of many tribes. Disease killed off thousands of Indians. Fishing as a way of life was replaced by logging, building and other forms of menial labor. Alcohol was introduced to the Indians. The long-house form of community life disappeared. In many areas, the culture was so uprooted that anthropologists and sociologists today are having trouble reconstructing the original tribal life-style. The Duwamish tribe, for instance, was located in almost the exact area where Seattle was originally settled. Their culture was totally obliterated. They received no land, and no longer exist as a distinct tribal unit today.

This imposition of language and culture is still resented in many ways. The Indians still live on reservations, and have tried to recover their cultural heritage. Conflicts remain regarding the rights of Indians to hunt and fish in the same manner as their ancestors. A strong area of conflict is the right of Indians to gill net salmon in the ocean and streams surrounding the Seattle area. Some tribes have been attempting to reestablish their pagan festivals honoring the salmon god, which was the central figure in many religious ceremonies.

3. What were the religious practices of ancient peoples on the site?

The Salish Indian group is on the southern end of the so-called "totem tribes." Their religious practices and beliefs are similar to the practices of most native groups up through the Alaskan coast. The religious leader of the community was the shaman, who was held to have great powers in the areas of blessing, cursing and healing. The shaman's position was validated by an initial encounter with a spirit guide, whose identity was kept secret. Shamans included both men and women, and the power was not necessarily passed along through family lines. The key and validating feature of the shaman was the initial spirit encounter.

The spirit encounter was not limited to the shaman. "Ordinary" people also sought out a spirit guide to help them go through life. Often, the spirit guide would lead them into a specific vocation, such as boat making. Most skilled craftsmen were assumed to have a spirit guide. The spirit guide generally appeared in the form of an animal. One example is that of a wood carver, whose spirit guide appeared in the form of a woodpecker. Whenever the person heard the sound of the woodpecker, they perceived that the spirit was nearby and was watching over their work.

A spirit guide was usually encountered through a time of prayer and fasting. The persons would ceremonially cleanse themselves, deprive themselves of food, and seek an encounter with the spirit world. Often they entered a trancelike state in which they met their spirit guide.

Salish gods are perceived of as somewhat impersonal and far off. Much of the benefit that has been given to humans (such as fire, tools and so on) was through the trickster who is pictured as either the raven or the coyote. The trickster gives people things they are not supposed to have. God is not necessarily friendly, but the deceiver is.

The main religious ceremony of the year centered around the return of the salmon. The Indians had great respect for the salmon, as the salmon was one of their main food sources. The first salmon would be ceremonially carried back to the village and there through a special ritual they would thank the spirits for the return of the fish.

Another ceremonial act that is not necessarily religious but was extremely important was the potlatch. In a potlatch, the host would have a great party for the invited guests featuring both feasting as well as lavish gift giving. This ceremonial act was validated by giving. Two main reasons for the potlatch were: (1) self-glorification—the host demonstrates his family wealth and position; and (2) the requirement of return gifts. Return gifts were the "catch" to the potlatch. To save face and maintain family glory the guests would have to offer a similar party and give bigger and better gifts. Because of this, the rich got richer and the poor got poorer. In another form of the potlatch, instead of giving gifts, the host would destroy his possessions in order to show his greatness. Instead of sharing, the person would destroy. This destruction could even include killing or maiming slaves.

A final area of religious practice relates to the dead. The spirits of ancestors were greatly feared. The tribes were very careful in the burial and honoring of the dead, so that their spirits would not return to haunt the tribe. One belief is that speaking the name of a dead person caused them "unrest" in the grave. Therefore, it may have been considered a great threat to Chief Seattle to have the city named after him, because each time the name was spoken it would affect him in his afterlife. Often the burial sites were adorned with carvings and fetishes, which in my opinion look hideous and fierce.

4. Was there a time when a new religion emerged?

Not as far as I could tell. Anthropologists speculate that shamanism came from Asia and was the dominant form of Indian religion until the arrival of Christianity.

5. Under what circumstances did the gospel first enter the city?

In 1852, Bishop Demers held the first religious ceremony in the town, almost everyone being in attendance. In the same year, the Reverend Benjamin Close, a Methodist, held the first Protestant services in the settlement of Seattle. The Reverend

Demers was going to Fort Victoria, and Close lived in Olympia, and so these were simply visitation services.

The first full-time resident minister arrived in the fall of 1853. The Reverend David Blaine and his wife, Catherine, established the first church, a Methodist Episcopal congregation. They were welcomed and sponsored by Arthur Denny, who provided their initial housing, and who with his wife made up two-thirds of the initial congregation. This was the only church in the area for more than 10 years.

The Blaines did not make a deep and lasting impression on Seattle. According to the standards of eastern United States, Seattle was not a religious community. One clear problem with the Reverend Blaine was his attitude toward the Indian population. In a letter home he basically says that the Indians are beyond help because of (1) the language barrier; (2) their sinful behavior; and (3) their societal context.

From early 1856 through late 1860, Seattle had no resident minister. Church meetings were held quarterly in the Methodist church. In late 1860, the Reverend Daniel Bagley arrived from Oregon. He was a church planter, having planted 20 churches in Oregon and Washington. Bagley became one of the main second-generation city founders, and was instrumental in getting the first university started in Seattle (later the University of Washington). He was also a Freemason, along with several other city founders.

Additional ministers began arriving in 1865, when the Episcopalians from Olympia came to town and started a congregation. The Presbyterians arrived in 1866 in the form of the Reverend George Whitworth, who also became an industrial leader with the Reverend Bagley. At this early stage, the churches worked together well—two churches and four pastors represented four denominations. So two pastors worked in each church and alternated preaching duties, having basically no problems. The Catholics arrived in 1867, the Congregationalists and Baptists in 1869. The Baptist minister was the Reverend Edward Hanford, who was one of the great early spiritual leaders of Seattle.

Chief Seattle, the famous Indian leader, in his treaty signing speech, probably best articulates the position of the Indians regarding the "white man's God." Part of his speech was: "Your God is not our God! Your God loves your people and hates mine. He folds His strong protecting arms lovingly about the pale face...but He has forsaken His red children, if they really are His. Our God, the Great Spirit, seems also to have forsaken us." If anything, Chief Seattle expresses the inability of the church to present a true picture of God. Unfortunately, what the Indian saw was the God of the greedy, murdering, stealing, white men. They saw the invasion of the whites as a spiritual power struggle, which the Great Spirit had lost.

6. Has the national or city government ever disintegrated?

Yes, in a manner of speaking. Early city government was extremely corrupt. Henry Yesler, a prominent sawmill owner, was in a strong position of power for many of the early years, and used his influence to make money for himself at the expense of the city. This early corruption required that the city basically start over again after Yesler was out of a position of power. Yesler's swindling techniques had pushed the city to the brink of bankruptcy several times.

7. What has been the leadership style of past governments?

The government style of Seattle has generally focused around the philosophy of business first. In many ways, business has ruled government, there being little regulation of business. As previously mentioned, Henry Yesler for many years had the power position in Seattle government. In this position he was neither honest nor fair. He favored business over people, and his own business over other businesses. If someone proposed something that might benefit someone else and not him, he often vetoed the project or siphoned off the funds for other uses. Yesler is the early epitome of wealth and riches perverting justice, fairness and concern for people.

The period between 1900 and 1920 was one of the key times for shaping the city of Seattle. The decision was put before the voters whether to close the city of Seattle to gambling, drinking and prostitution houses. The vote went back and forth, but in the end, Seattle remained an open city, although not as open as it had been during the Yukon gold rush. At that time, the government and police force were plagued by graft and corruption.

8. Have there ever been wars that affected this city?

The primary effect of war upon Seattle has been economic prosperity. In many ways the two world wars helped prosper the industries of shipbuilding, airplanes, manufacturing and shipping.

9. Was the city itself the site of a battle?

One minor Indian battle occurred around 1856. The city of Seattle was put on alert, and a brief skirmish took place. Two city residents were killed, and many more Indians. The Indians launched the attack because of broken treaty promises by the white men. Historians believe that Seattle survived this battle only because the Indians were too slow in attacking, allowing the city to send for help. It arrived in the form of a Navy gunboat, which shelled the Indians and accounted for most of the Indian casualties.

10. What names have been used to label the city, and what are their meanings?

The Emerald City. This is best understood as referring to the environment of Seattle. Seattle has an abundance of evergreen trees, as well as surrounding lakes and mountains. The name reflects this lush aspect of Seattle; however, the title could also represent the wealth and riches of the area.

11. Why was the city originally settled?

Indians appear to have originally settled in Seattle because of the wealth of natural resources and the climate. Although the sky is often overcast, the temperature rarely drops below freezing for any length of time in the winter, and snow is infrequent and short lived.

White people came with the purpose of making money through trade. The early traders came on their way to China and traded for sea otter skins. They discovered they could make a fortune selling otter skins in China. Early settlements focused on trading with the Indians to get otter skins and then taking the skins to China. This lasted a relatively short time as the otters were nearly driven to extinction.

Arthur Denny and his party (the founders) came looking for a place to establish a port where they could open trade routes to the Far East. They were business people looking for a prime location to make money. They found this location to be a little swampy island with a deep water harbor and ready access to timber and other natural resources. Much of their original trade, however, was with San Francisco, which was the main town involved in the California gold strike. Seattle was a ready location for harvesting and shipping timber, which San Francisco desperately needed.

Later arrivals generally came with the idea of getting rich. The city was composed primarily of middle-class people. Many of these did become rich, and thus the upper class was very middle class in its roots. Business opportunities abounded in timber, manufacturing and farming. The city grew at an amazing rate until the 1920s when growth leveled off until the boom years of World War II.

12. Did the city have a founder? What was his dream?

Seattle was founded by Arthur Denny, Carson Boren and William Bell. This group located the deep water channel and plotted the original town location. Charles Terry originally chose to settle across the bay at Alki, but soon traded some land and moved to Seattle proper.

The dream of Arthur Denny was to establish a secure family home. He was concerned about building a solid community for the future. His primary concern was not in getting rich, but in having a solid community with a business base and a strong population. Denny was a man of great integrity and honesty, and was well respected in the community. No alcohol was allowed in his businesses or on his land. He was a major factor in the establishment of schools (including the University of Washington), as well as the first church. He was considered a man of his word by all people, including the Indians. However, it is interesting to note that no one writes about liking Denny. He was respected, honest and upright—but not well liked.

However, a strong negative feature of Denny, which I believe is reflected in Seattle today, must also be mentioned. Denny for all his values and integrity seems to have been basically a man of inaction regarding moral issues. As far as I can tell, he made no strong stands against the moral wrongs that were regularly occurring around him. He basically minded his own business. This attitude seems to have permeated the city in that day, and continues on today.

13. As political, military and religious leaders have emerged, what did they dream for themselves and for the city?

An important vision was for a utopian city for the upper-middle class. This was evident in the division of Seattle and the rebuilding and expansion of the city following the fire of 1889. From almost the start, Seattle was divided into the good and bad sections. The bad section was located south of Skid Road, and was the home of the drunk, the poor, the hungry, the destitute and the minority. It was the home of crooks, pimps and prostitutes. The "respectable" people lived in the good section of town.

The people in political power generally supported the "good" people—the upper-middle-class businesspeople. Early city design and expansion focused on improving their lives and conditions. Streetcars ran into the good locations of town. Parks were planned, streets graded and improved. But the recipient of these improvements was the upper-middle class.

14. What political, economic and religious institutions have dominated the life of the city?

Political groups, businesspeople and liberal-minded groups have had the most dominance in Seattle. There was a brief period of blue (i.e. righteousness) laws in the early 1900s, mostly in an effort to clean up the Skid Road area, but these were ignored for the most part and eventually repealed.

Labor unions have been a strong influence since the 1930s, and several major strikes have taken place over the years. The labor unions and the strong business-oriented government have tended to produce conflict over time. The businesses have tended to exploit labor, and the unions have in many ways hurt business through strikes, anti-minority contracts and so on. The unions have also been subject to considerable abuse by leaders, including perceived sellouts as well as graft and corruption.

Economic dominance has changed over time. The original economic base was timber, the Yesler sawmill being the front-runner in this area. In some ways, that continues today; Weyerhaeuser lumber products is located near Seattle and employs approximately 40,000 people.

Shipping and trade was and is a major industry. Much of this trade has been with the Far East and with Alaska. Seattle is the major stopping point for most of the trade with Alaska, and this has been very important, especially during the time of the Alaska gold strike. Today, approximately 17 percent of all jobs are tied to import-export businesses.

The major economic force, however, is the Boeing Company. Boeing provides approximately 100,000 local jobs in a variety of industries, mostly aerospace. The economy of Seattle is strongly tied to Boeing, and seems to follow the direction of Boeing. Perhaps an area of concern here is reliance upon Boeing instead of reliance upon God.

Religiously, no dominant institutions have emerged. However, the Freemasons should be mentioned. Freemasonry has been present in Seattle from the beginning. Several of the early leaders in both business and church were Freemasons, including Doc Maynard and the Reverend Daniel Bagley. Bagley was a lifelong Mason, and had achieved the Royal Arch level of Masonry prior to moving to Seattle. In Seattle, he was elected the Grand Master of the first lodge the year after the lodge was founded.

15. What has been the experience of immigrants to the city?
Generally, the experience has been good. The founding fathers of Seattle readily accepted new people, and any anti-Irish or anti-Jewish mentalities have not surfaced, due to two factors: (1) few large immigrants groups have settled in Seattle (except Scandinavians in Ballard); (2) most, if not all, immigrants tended to end up in the slums, which have been a part of the city since the 1880s. In the late 1800s, a desire to curb Chinese immigrants may have surfaced, which may be spiritually significant.

16. Have there been any traumatic experiences such as economic collapse, race riots or an earthquake?
The early economy of Seattle was tied to San Francisco. When San Francisco diminished after the gold rush, so did Seattle. A major economic collapse occurred in the 1890s, which basical-

ly destroyed the banks of Tacoma. The Seattle banks survived, however, by pooling resources. Later economic scares were generally related to Boeing layoffs, especially in the early 1970s.

Race riots (as performed by nonwhite groups) occurred in 1968, when the black population was in a severe time of transition. Gangs calling themselves the "Blacks" and the "Whites" were present on the streets and often in conflict with one another.

Major fires plagued Seattle, Spokane and Ellensburg in 1889. In each place, the business district was virtually destroyed. Seattle and Spokane recovered, Ellensburg did not. The downtown region of Seattle gained much of its current appearance after this fire.

I found two recorded earthquakes of significant magnitude. In April of 1949 and 1965, serious earthquakes shook Seattle. The second one measured 7.0.

In 1980, Mount Saint Helens, which is fairly close to Seattle, had a major volcanic eruption that removed the top of the mountain. This attracted massive attention in Seattle.

17. Did the city ever experience the birth of a socially transforming technology?

Possibly. Although airplanes were not invented in Seattle, the advances made by Boeing in the aerospace industry might be considered socially transforming.

18. Has there ever been the sudden opportunity to create wealth such as the discovery of oil or a new irrigation technology?

Without a doubt. However, these opportunities are generally related to trade.

Seattle's first trade opportunity was with San Francisco, which needed timber. A second opportunity came with the Alaska and Fraser River gold strikes. The miners going north generally passed through Seattle both coming and going, and spent large amounts of money in the process.

19. Has there ever been religious conflict among competing religions or among Christians?

At this point, I have found no such conflict. The early churches were often multidenominational. At one point, Seattle had four ministers from different denominations, and only two churches. They resolved the issue by sharing duties instead of building more churches.

20. What is the history of relationships among the races?

Appalling. This is a major area of trouble in the city of Seattle, and needs much repentance and prayer. For the most part, until the later 1900s, most minorities have been centered in the international district or the slums south of what was known as Skid Road. The history of this region is important to understand. This was the area where the first brothels and bars were built. This was the section of town where gambling, drinking and prostitution were rampant. And this was the area where minorities were expected to live by the unwritten laws of Seattle society.

Indians

Prior to the arrival of the whites the Indians experienced frequent wars and raiding among themselves. The purpose of these wars was to capture slaves, who were symbols of wealth and status. Slaves had essentially no rights. They could be used as prostitutes, killed, maimed or whatever the owner desired. The fiercer tribes tended to be located to the north in British Columbia. Local Indians lived in fear of these groups of Indians who often came to their territories on raiding missions.

When the whites arrived, they immediately began to exploit the Indians (with the exception of the Jesuit priests). Initially, they traded for furs, and then when Seattle was founded they began to use Indians as a labor source. Of course they were paid, but it was much less than what a white person would have been paid. The whites for all intents and purposes, took whatever land they wanted, and put the Indians on reservations "for their own good." They promised the Indians a place to live, education, help in establishing businesses, medical assistance, fishing rights and so on. The whites never met most of these terms, and still do not fully meet them today.

Indian slave women were poorly treated. The Indians already had fairly lax sexual standards, and white men found little trouble in sexually exploiting Indian women. John Pennell came to the Seattle area from San Francisco in 1861 and established the beginnings of the Skid Road section of Seattle. He established bars and brothels to cater to the large population of single men who had money to spend and wanted female companionship and entertainment. His female "workers" were Indian women (until some professional prostitutes from San Francisco came up in the 1870s) who were either slaves purchased from local tribes or women lured to the area with the promise of a place to stay, food to eat and clothing. What they found was a life of prostitution, exploitation and abuse. Very little, if anything, was done to stop Pennel's establishments.

Justice was also denied the Indians. When Bad Jim, an Indian, was lynched, the white lynchers were brought to trial. One of the white people being tried sat on the grand jury that was indicting them (he stepped down as they indicted him). When one white person pleaded guilty, the court quickly appointed a lawyer to plead not guilty for him. After a brief "trial," all of the white men were acquitted of a crime of which they were clearly guilty. On the other hand, when Indians were brought to trial they were generally either lynched or found guilty, regardless of the evidence. Chief Leschi was tried and hung for murder on very marginal evidence, in spite of many of his friends (including Doc Maynard) arguing for his innocence.

Afro-Americans

Afro-Americans have an interesting relationship to Seattle. Seattle began to grow after the Civil War, and was by law in an antislavery territory, so slavery was never an issue. Seattle was antislavery, however, it was also antislave, in that black people were not welcome and were afforded very few rights. Seattle was a "white" town. The blacks who did come found that they could really only live in one area, that being the slums south of Skid Road, the Seattle ghetto. As time progressed, they received very few rights in the city. Union contracts excluded blacks until this was broken by the courts in the 1940s.

Chinese

The Chinese faced their time of abuse in the late 1880s. They were originally imported as cheap labor to build the railroads and perform other dangerous and menial tasks. After the railroads were built, the Chinese began to move into the established cities, including Seattle, where they settled in the Skid Road slums. Many white people perceived this as threatening to their jobs, and decided to do something about the Chinese workers. After weeks of meetings and agitation, the crowds decided to act. They packed up the Chinese and began to load them on a steamer to San Francisco. Then a judge got involved and stopped the affair, and eventually things settled down.

What is appalling is the people who were and were not involved in the Chinese expulsion from Seattle. Only one church, a Methodist Episcopal, came out with a statement opposing the anti-Chinese movement. Eventually, the court ruled that the Chinese could not be expelled, but several hundred left the area, mainly because of fear.

SECTION II: DISCERNING SEATTLE, BEV KLOPP

I am greatly appreciative of Mark McGregor's research to lay the foundation for the spiritual mapping of Seattle. Many of the facts he has uncovered will give future direction to intercessors throughout Seattle as they continue praying for our dear city.

Before Mark's research, some of us had already been interceding for the Emerald City. I am happy to report that the number of humble believers called by God to immerse themselves in the spiritual battle for Seattle and the Pacific Northwest is increasing rapidly. To see God's Kingdom poured out in Seattle, we need more intercessors and we need more information about our city and region. This combination will provide us a clearer picture of Seattle as it really is, not as it appears to be, to use the words of George Otis, Jr.

The thoughts I am sharing here emerge from untold hours of often agonizing and heartrending prayer over our city. I realize that we do not have final answers to all the spiritual powers of darkness that seek to keep Seattle in bondage, so what I share must be seen as coming from a people in process. At the same time, we cannot hide the fact that we do believe spiritual progress is being made.

REDEMPTIVE PRAYERS

As leaders and intercessors, we have been led by the Lord to attempt to translate the kind of historical research Mark McGregor has done into redemptive prayers, effective spiritual warfare, and restorative outreach that will break through strongholds. We are encouraged by seeing some results in the awakening of the Church and the salvation of the lost. We have cried out from 2 Chronicles 7:4-16 as we have united in prayer and repentance. Like Elijah, we believe we see the small cloud of God's presence preparing to release a greater outpouring of the Holy Spirit on an areawide scale.

As the largest city in the state of Washington, Seattle is in many ways a modern, pagan frontier of independence, where every possible counterfeit worship of the Godhead and perversion of the Father's love is evidenced. The master of deceit has long kept Seattle and the Pacific Northwest oppressed under spiritual darkness but, today, he trembles, exposed before the pure in heart who are willing courageously and sacrificially to obey God. At this hour, I believe the Lord stands with His foot upon the state of Washington, ready to display His power in glorious acts of compassion.

Washington state is known as being the least-churched state in the nation, as well as one of the world's three major centers for the New Age movement. Less than a year ago, Washington was a focus of national attention as it had two major initiatives on the ballot, one strengthening the rights for abortion, and one on euthanasia. The state was viewed by many in the national media as a leading force in both of these areas. Also, Seattle is regarded by many as one of the most liberal cities in America. It has one of the largest homosexual communities on the West Coast.

As Mark McGregor indicates, the lives of the earliest inhabitants, the American Indians, and the founding leaders of Seattle reflect ungodly ties that can often be traced to their pagan roots and sinful alliances with the enemy. For example, the American Indians are of Mongolian heritage who came from Siberia and the Far East, and have entrenched practices of shamanism and goddess worship.

In the past, many of the Indian tribes in the Northwest allied themselves with the powers of darkness through contact with ancestral spirits. They performed personal rituals for inducing spirit guides to help them gain wealth and slaves, as well as success in war, hunting, fishing and curing illnesses. Many of these precious people were driven deeper into their shamanistic roots through hardships, the plundering of other tribes, and the exploitation and disillusionment that came as a result of the treatment of the early white settlers. This is reflected in Chief

Seattle's speech, "Your God loves your people...He has forsaken His red children, if they are really His."

It is true, as Mark McGregor says, that Chief Seattle's famous speech expressed his despair that the white's God seemed not to love the Indians. How else could he interpret the greed, the murder, the abuse and the injustice of many of our first settlers? But Chief Seattle also went on to say that the "invisible dead" of his tribe would remain. He said, in the same speech, "Our religion is the traditions of our ancestors—the dreams of our old men, given...by the Great Spirit....At night...when the streets of your cities...will be silent...they will throng with the returning hosts."

Whites did not sin only against native Indians. McGregor points out that similar abuses are recorded in regard to the Asians and blacks through cheap labor, illegal acts and other injustices. Reactive sins and vengeance toward one another, instead of forgiveness and repentance, set the stage for further strongholds.

THE IMPOTENT CHURCH

Unfortunately, the church was not able to break through strongholds with the message of God's love partly because of its own misconceptions, worldliness, compromises and indifference. As a result, the lies of the enemy have been reinforced, setting up new "strongholds of the mind" as Cindy Jacobs would say, against one another and against the true knowledge of God's liberating truths. Greater divisions have resulted and the evil powers behind all of this have remained essentially unexposed. For example, the Indian nations in this area are separated and isolated in despair on their reservations around the state while the wealthy and powerful continue in their city "kingdoms" with their gods of materialism, hedonism, rationalism and intellectualism.

We are sensing that today Satan's blinding remains over the

minds of the unbelievers. There appears to be a "slumbering bewitchment" captivating the minds of both believers and unbelievers by way of religious deception and seduction, apathy, separation and disunity. It seems to point out that the evil forces mentioned in Ephesians 6 have established rights as a result of these entrenched patterns of sin and unholy alliances with the enemy.

Such alliances have given the enemy undeserved power and access to Washington and its people groups. This can be seen through the continuation of generational iniquities, the increase of the New Age movement, satanic rituals, and unjust laws, festivals and personal pacts. In the past, this was illustrated by unfair land treaties, broken agreements between the American Indians and the early settlers, social injustices against minorities, and the removal of prayer from schools. These agreements are spiritual decrees of rights, allowing the enemy to maintain the continuous entrenchment of strongholds. Today, the leaders in this area are becoming aware and alert to the spiritual knowledge and unity needed to break such strongholds.

SHOULD WE NAME THE POWERS?

We realize not all agree that we should probe deeply enough in our intercession to learn the proper names of the principalities and powers over a city such as Seattle. I do not insist that knowing the names is essential to effective spiritual warfare (but see Mark 5:9; Luke 8:30). Peter Wagner has discussed this issue in his book, *Warfare Prayer*, and I agree with his conclusion: "Although it is not always necessary to name the powers, if the names can be found, whether functional names or proper names, it is usually helpful for focusing warfare prayer."[2] I would not want to be dogmatic about this, but many of us who have been travailing in intercession for the city feel we have agreement on some of the identities of the chief principalities. Most are spirits specifically named in the Scriptures.

Some of the names we have found have come forth as relating to particular strongholds in this area. I name a few for their "fruit," which can help us connect the spiritual powers that control this area: Apollyon (Rev. 9:11) the destroyer, has its death and destruction, its spirit of divination and works of Jezebel, and its anti-Christ spirit of deception, rebellion, idolatry and covetousness; Beelzebub (Matt. 12:24) or the ruler of demons, has its control and manipulations, religious counterfeits of the gifts and doctrines of demons; Asmodeus (in the apocryphal Book of Tobit 3:8), has its religious seductions, greed and sexual perversions; Belial (2 Cor. 6:15), has its false prophets and shepherds, and unrighteous leaders of wickedness, lawlessness and false teachings. Added to this we have an Indian spirit called the "Great Spirit" in the Northwest with its shamanism and ancestral worship.

In addition, we feel there are spirits called Androgyny and the Dragon, the slayer of souls. Along with these come the destruction of people, distortions of God's love and truth, violence and sexual abuse against women and children, and perversions of every kind in male and female roles and relationships. They are linked with greed, pornography, witchcraft, racism and religious spirits. We also think we have identified a regional spirit on Mount Rainier, which has long been worshiped as "the most high" god through the avenues of Satan worship, goddess and mother-earth worship, shamanism, and New Age activities. Finally, we are dealing with a warring, pirating, jack-tar concept relating to unrighteous trade, unjust laws, and incoming drugs and opium tar.

HEALING STARTS WITH REPENTANCE

As intercessors, we have sought to push back the spiritual holocaust caused by these wicked spirits over Seattle. They have brought chaos, confusion and torment to our people for years, resulting in a death-strewn path. Through prayer, we are attempting to break the power and curses that keep people bound to past failures. We have prayed for the masquerade to be removed and for the sectarian spirit to be exposed with repentance. We have sought God's grace and mercy over past sins, and have asked God to bind up the wounds. We have cried out for God to break the patterns, the callousness and hardness of people, both Christians and non-Christians, by bringing forth repentant hearts that forgive and extend grace and mercy to one another.

Through repentance, cleansing, and breaking of sinful ties, these spirits must go. Writing new laws and establishing godly worship and loving relationships can further break the "rights" of these territorial spirits. Spiritual warfare and prophetic prayer actions such as Kjell Sjöberg describes (see chapter 4) can loosen the holds for a season, preparing minds to be open to the gospel and to the final deliverance that comes through personal repentance and godly living. As intercessors, we have fasted and prayed often and sought to bring healing. Step by step, the Holy Spirit has guided us in our prayer toward breaking down strongholds in the area.

TEARING DOWN STRONGHOLDS

The following are two examples of the many ways we have sought to bring needed changes through prayer and reconciliation.

Praying
Several years ago we began praying over the Pioneer Square area, which is the oldest part of the city. This part of Seattle was literally built upon its own ruins as a result of the fire that Mark McGregor describes. This provides a natural picture

that seems to reveal the spiritual condition of the city. As we prayed through the underground buildings, remembering the past corruption of the city and its founding leaders, our grief was heightened. We identified with their sins through our own roots of fallenness, and confessed our personal sins as well as the indifference, disunity and moral compromise of the church. We sought God's mercy and forgiveness using John 20:23, "If you forgive the sins of any, they are forgiven." We cried out for repentance and restoration for the church and the people of the city.

The warfare against Satan's blinding of minds rose easily in our hearts as the blatant evil and deception of the enemy was exposed. Using the principles of Jeremiah 1:10, we began to pull down and uproot as we confronted the spirits behind greed, opportunism, deceit, pride, rebellion, independence, revelry, harlotry, wantonness, perversity, drunkenness, addiction, pornography, sodomy, murder, racism, prejudice, despair, poverty, religious indifference, Masonic influence, liberalism, rivalry, strife, suspicion, self-seeking, self-exaltation, domination, injustice, alienation and oppression. We used the principles of 2 Corinthians 10:4-6 and began to cast down false arguments and beliefs contrary to God and His truths. Our faith rose as we proclaimed the lordship of Jesus Christ and prophetically declared the Word with songs over the darkness.

Repenting

In May 1992, Gateway Ministries International, which I serve, invited pastors and city leaders to a brunch for the purpose of repenting of our personal prejudices and the historical roots of racial wounding in this area. Almost every ethnic group was represented. We began with the original broken relationships between the American Indians and the early white settlers, and continued with each ethnic group. During this time, more than 200 women from around the state gathered for a 24-hour prayer vigil in the center of Seattle to pray for the city and the church leaders who were gathering. Forgiveness and repentance were also extended between the women of the various ethnic groups present. Repentance for the sins of past relationships between men and women also occurred. Awesome healing took place and seeds of renewal were sown.

SEATTLE'S REDEMPTIVE GIFTS

The Body of Christ in Seattle is beginning to unite. For us to have the greatest impact, we must increase our watchfulness

---

Through our repentance, the church shall have the power to impart effective intercession, and to preach with power. The church must arise to its inheritance, for today is the Lord's *kairos* hour to triumphantly enter our [Seattle's] gates.

---

now with citywide prayer vigils and a united strategy for outreach that brings repentance and reconciliation. Strongholds will be brought down as we love one another, and together lift up the name of the Lord Jesus. "And I, if I be lifted up from the earth, will draw all men unto me" (John 12:32, *KJV*).

Seattle is called to be a city on a hill that cannot be hidden—a refuge of light. It is to be a city that glorifies God through worship and praise, and through sharing spiritual and physical gifts with the nations. Seattle is to be a missionary city bringing the life and love of Jesus Christ to the multitudes, through praying, proclaiming and giving.

The spiritual forces behind strongholds that have affected Seattle and Washington state for centuries shall soon bow the knee as the church unites to reach the lost and hurting. The weakest of the weak, the poorest of the poor, and the most disillusioned and oppressed shall soon rise to defeat the enemy who has oppressed them from the earliest beginnings. Through our repentance, the church shall have the power to impart effective intercession, and to preach with power. The church must arise to its inheritance, for today is the Lord's *kairos* hour to triumphantly enter our gates.

■ REFLECTION QUESTIONS ■

1. Why is this chapter divided into two parts? Is this significant?
2. What is the meaning of the term "redemptive prayers"? How is this method of praying different from others?
3. In what ways can the church be an obstruction to the manifestation of God's power in a city? Is this the case with churches in your city?
4. How important do you think it is to discover the names of the territorial spirits over a city?
5. What role does repentance have in strategic-level spiritual warfare? Explore the ways serious repentance could be done in your city.

Notes
1. John Dawson, *Taking Our Cities for God* (Lake Mary, FL: Creation House, 1989), p. 85. Used by permission.
2. C. Peter Wagner, *Warfare Prayer* (Ventura, CA: Regal Books, 1992), p. 150.

Summary: Mapping Your Community

by C. Peter Wagner

MANY WILL BE ASKING: HOW DO I DO IT IN MY CITY? Because few Christian leaders today have much background in spiritual mapping, the answer to that question will not come easily. It is important not to fall into the trap of thinking this is some sort of magic that will work if we do things in the same manner as Victor Lorenzo or Bev Klopp. There is no one way to do spiritual mapping.

Having said that, I also realize guidelines can be helpful. This brief summary chapter is designed to provide some of those guidelines. In preparing it, I have gone through all the chapters of the book in which the contributors mention questions they ask or procedures they usually use when spiritually mapping a city or an area. I have also drawn upon some valuable material Cindy Jacobs prepared, but is not found in her chapter. Putting this all together gives us a systematized list of questions to ask when undertaking spiritual mapping. The list is neither complete nor final. You might want to add other questions. Some might not be useful to you at all. But it is a beginning.

There are many levels of spiritual mapping. Mapping could be done in your neighborhood or in your particular section of the city. Mapping could be done for the city as a whole, or for the city and its surrounding area, or for the state or the province, or for the entire nation. Some will want to map clusters of nations. For the sake of simplicity, I am going to assume we are mapping a city and I will word the questions accordingly. But the same questions obviously will apply to virtually any geographical area.

The first step is to *gather* the information; the second step is to *act* on the information. By this I do not mean to imply that all of the first step has to be done before the second step can begin. They can and should operate simultaneously. But the prayer action will be more effective if it is based on solid information.

STEP ONE: GATHERING THE INFORMATION

Following the lead of contributors such as Harold Caballeros, I am going to divide the information-gathering phase into three parts: (1) historical research, (2) physical research, (2) spiritual research. Whether you would want to assign this to three separate teams as Caballeros does is up to you. But it does have some advantages if personnel is available.

HISTORICAL RESEARCH

I. THE HISTORY OF THE CITY

A. The Founding of the City

1. Who were the people who founded the city?
2. What was their personal or corporate reason for founding the city? What were their beliefs and philosophies? What was their vision for the future of the city?
3. What is the significance of the original name of the city?
   - Has the name been changed?
   - Are there other names or popular designations for the city?
   - Do these names have meanings? Are they linked to religion of any sort? Are they demonic or occultic names? Do they signify blessing? Curse? Do they highlight the city's redemptive gift? Do they reflect the character of the people of the city?

B. The Later History of the City

1. What role has the city played in the life and character of the nation as a whole?
2. As prominent leaders have emerged in the city, what was their vision for their city?
3. Have any radical changes taken place in the government or political leadership of the city?
4. Have there been significant or sudden changes in the economic life of the city? Famine? Depression? Technology? Industry? Discovery of natural resources?
5. What significant immigration has occurred? Was there ever an imposition of a new language or culture on the city as a whole?
6. How have immigrants or minorities been treated? How

have races or ethnic groups related to one another? Have city laws legitimized racism of any kind?

7. Have city leaders broken any treaties, contracts or covenants?
8. Have any wars directly affected the city? Were any battles fought in the city? Was there bloodshed?
9. How has the city treated the poor and oppressed? Has greed characterized city leaders? Is there evidence of corruption among political, economic or religious leaders and institutions?
10. What natural disasters have affected the city?
11. Does the city have a motto or slogan? What is its meaning?
12. What kinds of music do the people listen to? What is the message they receive from that music?
13. What five words would most people in the city use to characterize the positive features of their city today? What five words would they use for the negative features?

II. HISTORY OF RELIGION IN THE CITY

A. Non-Christian Religion

1. What were the religious views and practices of the people who inhabited the area before the city was founded?
2. Were religious considerations important in the founding of the city?
3. Have any non-Christian religions entered the city in significant proportions?
4. What secret orders (such as Freemasonry) have been present in the city?
5. What witches' covens, satanist groups or other such cults have operated in the city?

B. Christianity

1. When, if ever, did Christianity enter the city? Under what circumstances?
2. Have any of the early or later Christian leaders been Freemasons?
3. What role has the Christian community played in the life of the city as a whole? Have there been changes in this?
4. Is Christianity in the city growing, plateaued or declining?

C. Relationships

1. Has there been conflict between religions in the city?
2. Has there been conflict between Christians?
3. What is the history of the church splits in the city?

PHYSICAL RESEARCH

1. Locate different maps of the city, especially the older ones. What changes have taken place in the physical characteristics of the city?
2. Who were the city planners who designed the city? Were any Freemasons?
3. Are there any significant discernible designs or symbols imbedded in the original plan or layout of the city?
4. Is there any significance in the architecture, location or positional relationship of the central buildings, especially those representing the political, economic, educational or religious powers in the city? Did Freemasons lay any of the cornerstones?
5. Has there been any historical significance in the particular plot of land upon which one or more of these buildings are located? Who originally owned this land?

6. What is the background of the city's parks and plazas? Who commissioned and funded them? What significance might their names have?

7. What is the background and possible significance of the statues and monuments of the city? Do any reflect demonic characteristics or glorify the creature rather than the Creator?

8. What other artwork is featured in the city, especially on or in public buildings, museums or theaters? Look especially for sensual or demonic art.

9. Are there any prominent archaeological sites in the city? What meaning might they have?

10. What is the location of highly visible centers of sin such as abortion clinics, pornographic bookstores or theaters, areas of prostitution, gambling, taverns, homosexual activities, etc.?

11. Where are areas that concentrate greed, exploitation, poverty, discrimination, violence, disease or frequent accidents?

12. Where are locations of past or present bloodshed through massacre, war or murder?

13. Does the position of trees, hills, stones or rivers form any apparently significant pattern?

14. Do certain landmarks of the city have names that would not glorify God?

15. What is the highest geographical point in the city and what is built or located there? This can be a statement of authority.

16. Which zones or sectors or neighborhoods of your city seem to have characteristics of their own? Attempt to discern areas of the city that seem to have different spiritual environments.

SPIRITUAL RESEARCH

A. Non-Christian

1. What are the names of the principal deities or territorial spirits associated with the city past or present?
2. What are the locations of high places, altars, temples, monuments or buildings associated with witchcraft, occult, fortune-telling, satanism, Freemasonry, Mormonism, Eastern religions, Jehovah's Witnesses and the like. Do these form any patterns when plotted on a map?
3. What are the sites of pagan worship from the past, even before the city was founded?
4. What are the different cultural centers that might contain art or artifacts connected with pagan worship?
5. Has any city leader knowingly dedicated himself or herself to a pagan god or a principality?
6. Were any known curses placed by the original inhabitants on the land or people who founded the city?

B. Christian

1. How have God's messengers been received by the city?
2. Has evangelism been easy or hard?
3. Where are the churches located? Which of them would you see as "life giving" churches?
4. What is the health of the churches in the city?
5. Who are the Christian leaders considered as "elders of the city"?
6. Is it easy to pray in all areas of the city?
7. What is the status of unity among Christian leaders across ethnic and denominational lines?
8. What is the view of city leaders toward Christian morality?

C. Revelational

1. What are the recognized, mature intercessors hearing from God concerning the city?
2. What is the identity of the ranking principalities seemingly in control of the city as a whole or certain areas of the city's life or territory?

STEP TWO: ACTING ON THE INFORMATION

An advantage of having several contributors in a book such as this is that they provide glimpses of several different approaches to strategic-level spiritual warfare. We have seen Cindy Jacobs lead the pastors of Resistencia in repentance. We have seen Kjell Sjöberg's friend infiltrate a Swedish occultic organization and observed Harold Caballeros find the strongman's name on a certain page in the Guatemala newspaper. We have seen Bob Beckett drive oak stakes into the ground at the gateways to Hemet. As well, we have seen Victor Lorenzo join in a human cross in the center of the plaza in La Plata, and Bev Klopp repent in Seattle's underground buildings. All of them found some advantage in the methods they used, but none of them claim that others should do it their way.

Through prayer, God will show leaders, city by city, what action is most appropriate for their particular situation. Meanwhile, there are some general rules for ministering to a city through strategic-level spiritual warfare. Those who have read the first book in this series, *Warfare Prayer*, will be familiar with the rules for taking a city, which I explained there. For the benefit of those who have not read it or those who have forgotten, I will simply list the six rules without further explanation:

Rule 1: The Area

Select a manageable geographical area with discernible spiritual boundaries.

Rule 2: The Pastors

Secure the unity of the pastors and other Christian leaders in the area and begin to pray together on a regular basis.

Rule 3: The Body of Christ

Project a clear image that the effort is not an activity simply of Pentecostals and charismatics, but of the whole Body of Christ.

Rule 4: The Spiritual Preparation

Assure the spiritual preparation of participating leaders and other Christians through repentance, humility and holiness.

Rule 5: The Research

Research the historical background of the city in order to reveal spiritual forces shaping the city. (This was covered in the first part of this chapter: "Gathering the Information.")

Rule 6: The Intercessors

Work with intercessors especially gifted and called to strategic-level spiritual warfare, seeking God's revelation of: (a) the redemptive gift or gifts of the city; (b) Satan's strongholds in the city; (c) territorial spirits assigned to the city; (d) corporate sin past and present that needs to be dealt with; and (e) God's plan of attack and timing.

■ REFLECTION QUESTIONS ■

1. This chapter contains 60 questions for spiritual mapping. Would some of the questions not apply to your city? Eliminate them.
2. Use the remaining questions for mapping your city. One or more persons may do this.
3. Plot what you find on actual city maps. Check your findings

with other Christian leaders to confirm the accuracy of your insights.

4. Form a team of intercessors to pray over the map and share their findings with participating Christian leaders.

5. Try to read the book *Warfare Prayer* by C. Peter Wagner before beginning actual spiritual warfare for your city.

INDEX

110 — 7 questions for spiritual mapping
111 — idols covnant to God/Satan who altars demands worship
127 — Yes!
135 — more intimate communication w/ God & Satan, more power, success
   (David
154 — learned to pray for people — emot., fin., pship., spiritual bondage
168 — unity
180 — salvation
181 — Silvoso's six steps
181-88 — Masons
190 — Do
198 — Ben Klopp — call for
198 — Taking atres for God — to question
   Dawson
198 — CA History?
220 — Jer 1:10 ?
224 — pastor info

15 - Read this book   restaurant
20   E2   41b 3   Stokes
25
30   10/40
34   us
35 - Dan 10
36 -
41 - get this
45 - Haiti
54 - cutters
56 - mapping - find redemptive gift of city
      goal is to restore God's glory
58 - KEY GOAL
61 - spiritual mapping / strongholds
63 - crucial ? = do they glorify God - 64 sv
65   "   " = 3 of them
79 - read
80 - stronghold def 93
81 - read
82 - "
84 - Jude - city wardens
86 - David   84 - 85 - 86
86 - curds
88 - forgiveness 89
98 - informed for prayer, concept for spiritual
      mapping
102 - G & 10wye
108 - sin
109 - intercession & sin   2 Cor 10:4-6